# DEEP IN THE HEART

# DEEP IN THE HEART

## A REMEDY FOR AN AILING TEXAS

# ROB MOSBACHER

THE SUMMIT GROUP
FORT WORTH, TEXAS

Published by The Summit Group
1227 West Magnolia
Fort Worth, Texas 76104

Cover Design: Barnes and Co., Inc.
Page Design: Jean Walker

*To my wife, Catherine.*
*She was the first to suggest that I do this book.*
*Her friendship, love, affection, support, and counsel mean*
*more to me than she will ever know.*

# Contents

# Preface

F irst and foremost, I want to thank Ron Lindsey. I first met Ron six years ago when he was serving as Governor Bill Clements's chief budget officer. He had worked in a variety of state government jobs, including a position on the staff of the legislative budget board. I was impressed by the fact that he understood not only the numbers, but also the multitude of programs behind those numbers.

When I was elected volunteer chairman of the board of the Texas Department of Human services, my first task was to help find a new commissioner, or staff head, for that agency. Although the board interviewed a number of candidates, we hired Ron Lindsey. We picked him because he understood state government and was willing to shake things up at an agency in desperate need of change.

I am very proud of our joint tenure at that huge bureaucracy. However, it was not always pleasant. We undertook the first outside management audit of the agency in more than twelve years and set about implementing many of the recommendations to reduce the layers of bureaucracy and improve efficiency. Anyone who dares to consolidate and reorganize a government agency is going to be shot at from all those whose empires or fiefdoms are threatened. Ron Lindsey took many of the slings and arrows aimed at me.

When I became a candidate for lieutenant governor, everything that occurred at the agency became a political issue, subject to the normal misrepresentation and half-truths that characterize campaigns today. While I expected no less, Ron Lindsey was often caught in the crossfire.

After the election, it became apparent that the new lieutenant governor was unwilling to work with Ron, due largely to his association with me. You cannot attempt to lead an agency the size of the Department of Human Services if your relationship with the lieutenant governor is strained. So Ron Lindsey stepped down and became a budget analyst for then-House Speaker Gib Lewis.

Ron served with distinction and honor as commissioner of the Texas Department of Human Services. Although he worked under the most trying of circumstances, he neither complained nor flinched.

As Ron's time with Speaker Lewis came to an end, I approached Ron about helping me with this book. Over the years, we often talked about the absurdities of our state government and the need for dramatic change.

I have been around politics and government for

more than twenty years. In that time, I have seldom met a more principled, dedicated public servant than Ron Lindsey. His commitment to this state and its people is truly remarkable.

The second person I want to acknowledge is Mark Sanders. He helped research, organize, and edit the book. His previous experience as a newspaper reporter was instrumental in keeping the text simple and straightforward. I appreciate his assistance.

Mary Kloss, my assistant and secretary, did a wonderful job of juggling different drafts and making constant changes without missing a stitch. Since we have worked together for nineteen years now, she can usually finish any sentence I start. I could not have done it without her.

I want to thank Herb Butrum for helping to find a Texas publisher that was interested in the project and willing to work with us. Herb also offered some editing suggestions and kept the project on track.

And finally, I want to express my appreciation to Charles Miller, Rusty Hardin, and Marie Oser for their input. I asked each of them to review parts of the book. Their observations were most helpful.

# Introduction

In 1841, when Sam Houston became president of the Republic of Texas for the second time, the financial condition of the fledgling nation was hurting. Boldly, Houston told the Texas Congress:

"There is not a dollar in the treasury. The nation is involved (sic) from ten to fifteen millions. The precise amount of its liability has not been ascertained. We are not only without money, but without credit, and for want of punctuality, without character."

It was not a great day in Texas history. But it was early evidence of the type of tough challenges this state has faced since before it joined the Union in 1845 or, as many of us were taught, when it annexed the United States. Some of those challenges threatened our very survival. Others were mere speed bumps on the road to economic growth and prosperity.

Throughout our history, we Texans have regarded government as a necessary evil which should be strictly limited in scope for fear that it could threaten our independence and freedom. So it is no wonder that for years, state government spending and programs were held to a minimum, focusing almost entirely on education, roads, and public welfare.

That began to change in the last half of this century. After one hundred years of financing state government without even a sales tax, much less an income tax, spending went through the roof.

Between 1968 and 1976, state spending doubled. Less than four years later, the budget doubled again and, believe it or not, doubled again by 1990. The spending plan most recently approved by the legislature puts Texas on a course to double its budget yet again by the end of this decade. All told, state government spending has increased more than a hundredfold since World War II and shows no sign of diminishing.

How could this happen, particularly in a state that prides itself on rugged individualism and stoic self-reliance instead of dependence on big government? That is one of the threshold questions I will answer in this remedy for Texas.

I also will show where the state is headed if we do not change our ways. Will spending continue to skyrocket and taxes with it? Is a personal income tax inevitable as some claim?

As important as where we have been, and where we are headed, is where we are today. What are we getting for the $35 billion we are spending this year on state government? Have dramatic increases in funding for public schools created similar increases in the quality of education? Has explosive growth in the cost of criminal justice made the streets safer? Has the immense expansion of welfare benefits made people more or less dependent on government?

Education, criminal justice, and health and human services make up over 70 percent of the entire current state budget. What do we have to show for the billions and billions of dollars spent, and the billions more yet to be spent?

For the past decade, every session of the state legislature has opened with the same basic question: Should we raise taxes to meet the ever-increasing budget needs of the state, or should we cut services? The most frequent answer has been a hodgepodge of both, with tax hikes exceeding budget cuts.

Are those the only options? There is no shortage of politicians who tell us that we have cut all the fat out of state government. Even John Sharp, the Comptroller of Public Accounts, claims we may have done all we can do. His auditors have identified some $6 billion in potential savings or new federal funds available to the state. But now it seems they have no more rabbits to pull out of the hat.

Perhaps that conclusion is what prompted Lieutenant Governor Bob Bullock to recommend adoption of a personal income tax in February 1991. Several months earlier in his campaign, he opposed such a tax, but that is another book altogether. He has since changed his mind.

Although Governor Ann Richards has consistently opposed a personal income tax, particularly in favor of the lottery, there is no indication that she has any idea how to kill the insatiable appetite of state government. Her much-publicized "New Texas" looks an awful lot like the old one. Some of the players in Austin have changed but the game is still the same, and it's getting more expensive every year for the taxpayers to play.

While the current patchwork system of tax collection, relying largely on sales and property taxes, is not particularly fair or efficient, it is infinitely better than the alternative—an income tax. It is not a question of whether compelling arguments can be made for spending more money on this problem or that, but rather a question of what we are getting for the money that is now being spent, and what we will be getting for the billions to be spent in the future. Until we can answer those questions, the idea of an income tax makes no sense at all.

There is an alternative to higher taxes and more government spending that apparently few, if any, of our leaders in Austin have considered. That alternative is to abandon the assumptions that serve as the basis for our state budget. Throw the baby out with the bath water and start over. That is what this book is all about. New ideas, a new direction, and new solutions.

It's also about cleaning up the political mess in our state capital. Those who travel the high road of integrity in Austin don't encounter a whole lot of traffic. Any attempt to pass creative, new solutions without changing the way state government business is conducted is destined to fail. We have to end the "same old-same old" in Austin.

Meaningful campaign finance and ethics reform, coupled with term limitations and massive government reorganization are all essential elements of establishing accountability. These are the means by which ordinary citizens can, and will, regain control of *their* government.

Finally, this book is about building a business climate in Texas that is second-to-none. As we approach the twenty-first century, economic competition among the fifty states of this nation, as well as among the nations of the world, will become increasingly intense. We must be ready for the challenge. Today, we are not.

We must marshal the courage and creativity to do things differently. Business leaders know they cannot keep pace unless they constantly change and improve the way they operate. The same should be true of our state government.

Texas is blessed with an abundance of strengths, most of which stem from the spirit and character of her people. With a leaner, more diversified private sector and an extraordinary opportunity to serve as the gateway to expanded trade with Mexico and beyond, Texas's future can be bright indeed. We will never realize our full potential as long as state government spending is out of control and accountability is lacking. The price for doing things the way they have always been done is simply unacceptable.

## Deep in the Heart

Yogi Berra once said, "If you come to a fork in the road, take it." We're there, and what follows is a road map.

# Part I:

# Identifying the Problems

# How Did We Get into This Mess?

I am the president of an independent oil-and-gas company founded in 1948 by my father. Like most people in our business, we have seen good times, and we've seen bad. When the industry was booming, we hired people and expanded our operations. At one point, we had more than two hundred employees.

But the last ten years have been tough on folks in the oil patch. I remember hearing about a sign nailed on a fence post that read: "Lost dog—right ear missing—left leg broken—tip of tail clipped off—recently spayed—answers to the name 'Lucky'."

While we have been luckier than most, when forced to we have tightened our belts and cut expenses. Today we employ about eighty people. That's the way the business world works. We flow with the economy. It is not the way state government works.

Back when my father started our business, the entire state budget was $319 million. Ross Perot could have paid for the whole thing with plenty left over.

This year, state government will spend $35 billion. That's an increase of more than one hundred times what was spent less than fifty years ago. Through good times and bad, regardless of the strength or weakness of our state's economy, our state government grew. That increase has been the most pronounced over the last thirteen years.

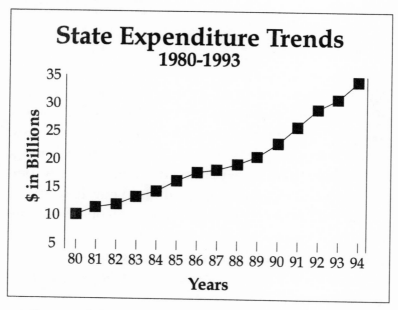

**State Expenditure Trends**
**1980-1993**

Some of that spending explosion certainly can be attributed to increases in population and inflation. In 1948, there were only seven million people living in Texas. Today, there are seventeen million. In 1948, a movie cost twenty-five cents, and a soda cost a nickel. Today, a movie costs $6.50, and a soda costs fifty cents. Some of our elected officials insist that population growth and inflation alone are responsible for the wild growth of state government. It just isn't so. If the cost of a movie or a Coke had increased as much as government spending has, today's movie ticket would cost more than $25, and the Coke would be going for more than $5. Clearly, something other than inflation is fueling growth in state government spending, although that's the song and dance we keep getting out of Austin.

Our state government has grown from a once-modest enterprise to the monster it is today primarily because of decisions and choices made over the years by various politicians and judges who have slid by shirking the public accountability that goes with their positions of responsibility.

Politicians established "entitlement" programs that require the state to spend money on everyone eligible for services, regardless of whether the money is available. Politicians created "dedicated funds," earmarking huge chunks of tax dollars for certain programs whether the programs need the money or not. In turn, state and federal judges imposed court orders that ultimately increased the amount of money we must spend on public education, prisons, and mental health facilities.

> **If the cost of a movie or a Coke had increased as much as government spending has, today's movie ticket would cost more than $25, and the Coke would be going for more than $5.**

Entitlement programs, dedicated funds, and court orders—those are the three forces driving the growth of state government spending. They are the primary reasons why state government spending is out of control, and they can each be traced to decisions made by elected or appointed leaders. In order to better understand how we got into this mess, it is essential to unmask these three spending villains.

## Entitlement Programs

**G**roucho Marx, when asked his opinion of modern American politics, said, "It is the art of looking for trouble, finding it everywhere, diagnosing it incorrectly, and applying the wrong remedies." That's probably the best explanation of how we got into the "entitlement" mess we find ourselves in today. It is the largest single piece in the budget equation.

When most of us hear the term "entitlement," we think of welfare, food stamps, Medicaid, or some other Great Society program passed by Congress. While those are indeed entitlement programs in which people who are poor enough become automatically eligible, they are not the only types of entitlement programs that exist.

Currently, three entitlements consume the lion's share of the state budget:
- public education
- health and human services
- criminal justice

Because administering these programs requires so many state employees, worker benefits such as health insurance and retirement plans have become the fourth entitlement program. Normally, we would not think of these programs—which provide such essential services—as entitlements, but that's exactly what they are.

> **I**n each case, anyone who meets the eligibility requirements for a certain program must be provided services even if there isn't a dime left in the state treasury to pay for it.

Here is the basic problem with these new entitlements: In each case, anyone who meets the eligibility requirements for a certain program must be provided services even if there isn't a dime left in the state treasury to pay for it. It's that simple. Prove you are eligible, and get the service—regardless of need or available funds, or even the effectiveness of the program offered.

Every school-age child in Texas is entitled to a public education. Every poor person is entitled to certain health and human services. And in 1995, thanks to decisions made by our current state leadership, criminal justice funding will become an entitlement as well.

The dramatic impact of entitlements can be shown by a quick look at the spending associated with public education, health and human services, criminal justice, and employee benefits. Between 1973 and 1983, those four programs grew at a rate *33 percent* faster than did the rest of state government. Over the next ten years, leading up to 1993, they grew *47 percent* more quickly than the rest.

Now, if these programs were small, it would be a matter of some concern, but not alarm. However, these entitlement programs are huge, comprising more than 70 percent of the entire state budget. That's billions and billions of our tax dollars.

> **T**he weakness here was that money was not tied to results or accomplishments, but only to the sheer number of students enrolled.

The largest component of entitlement spending is public education. Today, it is very common to read about the funding "crisis" in our schools. However, the first such crisis occurred not in this decade or the last, but shortly after World War II.

Huge differences existed in the amounts of funds available for education in rich, urban districts, as opposed to poor, rural ones. Teachers were underpaid, and the influx of "war babies"—now known as baby boomers—threatened to overwhelm the public school system. With the full support of Governor Beauford Jester, the legislature in 1947 established the Gilmer-Aiken Committee, named after Representative Claude Gilmer of Rocksprings and Senator A. M. Aiken of Paris.

That committee's report, entitled "To Have What We Must," served as the basis for passage two years later of the historic Gilmer-Aiken laws. Those laws established unequivocally that the primary responsibility for public education rested with the state, not local governments. In addition to strengthening the state board of education's authority and consolidating some three thousand school districts into a little more than one thousand, the laws also set minimum standards for all public schools to meet. Noble and worthy ideas, indeed.

But the Gilmer-Aiken laws also set the stage for the entitlement messes we have today. The amount of state money a local school district received to educate its children was tied directly to the number of kids in the school district, and little else. In other words, for every additional child that a school could claim, that school was entitled to more state aid. The weakness here was that money was not tied to results or accomplishments, but only to the sheer number of students enrolled. Hence, the creation of our largest state entitlement program.

In 1968, a federal lawsuit was filed on behalf of students in the Edgewood Independent School District in San Antonio contesting the manner of funding public schools. The Edgewood ISD argued that it was the state's responsibility to provide it and other poor districts with equal access to public funds. That suit made its way to the United States Supreme Court, where the district lost. But a subsequent lawsuit filed in the state courts was won.

Since 1989, Texas's system of school financing has been declared unconstitutional three separate times by our state supreme court. So what did lawmakers do? They pumped more money into the system. Despite abundant evidence that our school system is failing, the debate continues to center around the question of equal access to funds, or "equity," rather than results or the quality of education.

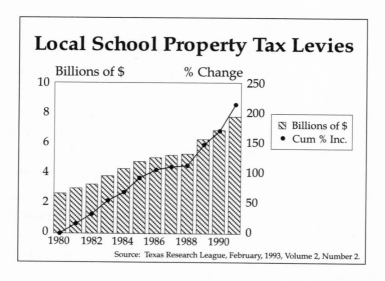

## Local School Property Tax Levies

Source: Texas Research League, February, 1993, Volume 2, Number 2.

During the 1980s alone, *state funding* for public-education programs more than doubled. In 1992, there were 3.2 million public school children in Texas, and biennial spending on education totaled $16.2 billion. And that's just state appropriations. In 1980, local school districts imposed a total of $2.5 billion in property taxes for education. By 1991, that had increased to $7.6 billion, a growth of 207 percent. Has the quality of public education in Texas improved 207 percent in the past ten years—or even 100 percent?

The dramatic increase in the cost of public education has not only caused property taxes to soar, but it has also been one of the dominant reasons why the state budget is out of control. Historically, about 50 percent of the state budget has been spent on education. Recently, that has declined as the legislature has shifted more of the funding burden to the local level and welfare spending has grown. Later, we'll consider what we have to show for this enormous investment in public education and what can be done to change things for the better. But now, here's a brief look at how spending has grown in the health and human services area.

> **D**espite abundant evidence that our school system is failing, the debate continues to center around the question of equal access to funds, or "equity," rather than results or the quality of education.

As I mentioned earlier, when one typically thinks of "entitlement" programs, welfare, food stamps, and Medicaid come to mind. While each of these programs was created by the Congress, they are funded by both the federal and state governments.

One hundred percent of the cost of food stamps is paid by the federal government, but each state is responsible for administering the program. In other words, the state pays for the bureaucrats. Welfare and Medicaid, on the other hand, are funded jointly, with the state picking up about 40 percent of the cost.

Although each state has some flexibility in determining who can take advantage of these programs, the federal government, in general, and Congress, in particular, really control eligibility. They determine who gets what.

Over the last several years, Congress has increased the cost of Medicaid enormously, by giving poor pregnant women and poor children greater access to the program. While this is a laudable goal, the states are obligated to pay their percentage of the cost, regardless of whether the states have the money in their budgets or not. So, in 1992 alone, combined state and federal spending for Medicaid in Texas increased by more than $1 billion. The same situation is occurring in all fifty states and shows every sign of continuing to skyrocket.

Health and human services now absorb more than 30 percent of the entire state budget, making it the second-largest program. Once again, while the state has some flexibility in running these programs, most of the control rests in Washington. Thus, not only does the Congress dictate who receives benefits, but it also controls a large chunk of the state's overall budget.

Public education and health and human services are the two largest entitlement programs in Texas, but there are others.

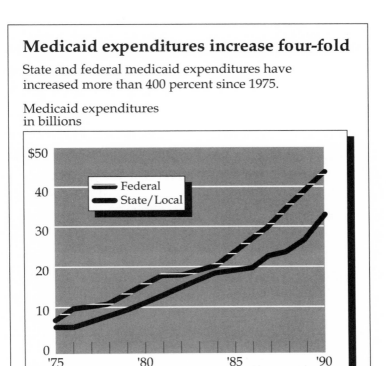

## Medicaid expenditures increase four-fold

State and federal medicaid expenditures have increased more than 400 percent since 1975.

Medicaid expenditures in billions

Source: Health Care Financing Administration.

# Dedicated Funds

L egendary Texas outlaws lived hard and died even harder, most remaining sullen and mean to the end. But not Green McCullough. When he was captured and led to a hanging tree in San Antonio, he openly admitted his guilt. As the noose slipped down around his neck, he told the crowd—some of whom he knew and had probably held up—"I've got to be hung, and I'm glad I'm going to be hung by friends."

Most modern Texas lawmakers who have looked honestly at what ails us would be happy to see a similar fate befall those who first came up with the idea of dedicating state funds—and they would have gladly provided the rope.

There are dozens of these funds which, in effect, are bundles of tax money dedicated by the state constitution, a statute, or a bond covenant to be spent on a particular purpose, and that purpose only. In 1991, the legislature instructed the state comptroller to consolidate some of the dedicated funds into a general operating fund. That left over three hundred in existence.

Among the largest of these funds are the state highway fund and the retirement systems. They are also the most sacred of sacred cows:

- The state highway fund was approved by Texas voters in 1946 and was instrumental in the development of the modern Texas economy. It helped integrate urban and rural communities and make this state a competitive economic force.

  Under the Texas Constitution, three-quarters of the revenue from gasoline and other motor vehicle fuel taxes, coupled with motor vehicle registration fees, go into this trust fund. That money is then spent on construction and maintenance of our highways and on the purchase of right-of-way. Part of it also goes to the

Department of Public Safety, and the remaining quarter is dedicated to public education.

The fund is reinforced by federal money and now makes up almost 10 percent of the entire state budget. It could well hit $7 billion by 1995.

- Employee and teacher retirement systems are also huge, dedicated funds. Under the Texas Constitution, the state is required to contribute an amount equal to at least 6 percent of public employees' and school teachers' salaries. However, because those retirement systems are so well funded, the legislature often postpones making regular contributions.

A third dedicated fund, of sorts, and one which will play an increasingly significant role in future state budgets, is *bonded indebtedness*. Bonds sold by the state are raising money to pay for much of the costs of building new prisons, as well as some schools. Worthwhile endeavors, but at a high cost.

In February 1993, Texas had approximately $8.8 billion in outstanding bonds and another $5.7 billion authorized but not issued. About 36 percent of issued bonds are general obligation bonds which require "the full faith and credit" of the state. Other than interest payments and new construction authorizations, those figures are not part of the $35-billion-a-year budget.

That debt service, paid from general revenue, has grown an average of 21.2 percent annually from 1986 to 1992, while general-revenue collections have increased only an average of 9 percent over that period. Again, we find ourselves in a boat filling with water faster than we can bail it out.

> **W**e are loading our children down with debt, just like those folks in Washington. What's more, we are tying the hands of future legislatures.

Although Texas remains relatively low in debt per capita, at least among the ten most populous states, it ranks second in local debt. The state debt service and total debt will steadily rise so long as the present trend continues of debt service increasing two and one-third times faster than general revenue. We are loading our children down with debt, just like those folks in Washington. What's more, we are tying the hands of future legislatures.

What is wrong with dedicated funds? Plenty. Designed to guarantee adequate money for important, needed programs, they now limit the flexibility of the legislature to control spending. In 1993, nearly two-thirds of all Texas agencies had their own special funds. Aside from the fact that we have perhaps five times as many agencies, commissions, and boards as we need, it is next to impossible to effectively control or cut spending at an agency that has its own dedicated fund.

Moreover, it limits the ability of the legislature to move funds from one program to another of greater importance. So, when the legislature gets down to struggling with how to make ends meet, it begins the debate with a big chunk of the budget totally untouchable. Any serious effort to address the budget problems of this state means breaking the stranglehold dedicated funds have on the budget.

# Court Orders

When President Franklin D. Roosevelt and his New Dealers proposed seizing oil pipelines and railroads in 1932, Texas reacted as if it had been invaded by a foreign army. Without a word to the Washington intruders, they opened oil wells all over the state and let flow six hundred thousand barrels of crude.

As "Baggage Truck" McGregor, Governor Ma Ferguson's representative, said, "Until hell freezes over, Texas will resist any effort on the part of the United States to interfere with its oil business." The move scuttled the New Deal plan.

Today, most Texans would gladly accept an equally severe show of displeasure if they thought it would get the modern invaders—the court system—out of the business of state government.

This is the third and final major cause of our budget mess: court orders affecting public schools, adult and juvenile criminal justice systems, and mental health and mental retardation facilities. I have already mentioned the famous *Edgewood ISD* case contesting funding between rich and poor school districts. State courts remain involved in questions of equity and adequacy of funding for the public schools, and will for the foreseeable future.

Then there is the case of the courts and the prisons. In 1971, the entire prison population in Texas was a little more than fifteen thousand. While we were slowly adding more prison cells, inmate David Ruiz filed a handwritten lawsuit against the head of the Texas Department of Corrections, W. J. Estelle. In it Ruiz claimed that conditions in Texas prisons violated provisions of the United States Constitution—specifically that he was being subjected to cruel and unusual punishment.

His lawsuit was combined with several others and heard in U. S. District Court by Judge William Wayne Justice. In December 1980, Judge Justice agreed with Ruiz and issued a series of requirements for sweeping change in the prison system.

In 1985 Justice and the state came to a settlement. Under the agreement, the state had to reduce by five thousand the prison population at twenty-six prison units. Furthermore, Justice imposed a cap on the number of inmates, prohibiting the state from operating any given prison at more than 95 percent of its capacity. In the meantime, other states were filling prisons well beyond 100 percent of capacity. That included California, which had operated prisons at up to 191 percent of planned capacity.

In any event, the court settlement forced the state to undertake the most ambitious prison construction program in the history of the country. Texas is leading the way because the court said it had to. Voters in 1987 approved a $500 million bond issue to build 15,000 additional prison beds. In 1989, another $333 million was approved for 11,100 more beds; and in 1991, another $643 million was OK'd for another 13,300 beds.

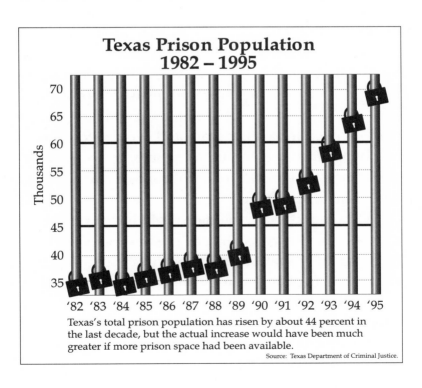

**Texas Prison Population 1982 – 1995**

Texas's total prison population has risen by about 44 percent in the last decade, but the actual increase would have been much greater if more prison space had been available.

Source: Texas Department of Criminal Justice.

Between 1992 and 1995, an estimated $1.3 billion will be spent on prison construction. The state will go from 55,000 prison beds to 107,429, including 10,000 state jail beds added to ease county jail overcrowding. And it all started with a court order.

> **W**ithout the order, the state could have undertaken a more orderly expansion of its prisons and considered more carefully some alternatives for preventing crime, rather than focusing entirely on trying to punish it.

All combined, this represents an increase in capacity of about 250 percent since 1980. Would Texas have needed that much prison space so soon in the absence of Judge Justice's order? No. The state could have placed more convicts in existing space and avoided the kind of revolving door we see today where, to avoid overcrowding, prisoners are made to spend only a fraction of their time behind bars.

Without the order, the state could have undertaken a more orderly expansion of its prisons and considered more carefully some alternatives for preventing crime, rather than focusing entirely on trying to punish it.

Despite this enormous increase in prison capacity, people do not feel significantly safer in their homes and neighborhoods than they did before. Fear of crime continues unabated. In chapter 4, I will lay out some specific proposals to alter the current pattern of criminal activity.

## How Did We Get into This Mess?

The following example of a court order allows us to fully appreciate the compelling role these mandates have played in the current budget situation. The Texas Department of Mental Health and Mental Retardation operates thirteen state schools for the mentally retarded. In 1974, *Lelsz v. Kavanaugh* was filed in federal district court on behalf of a small group of people in the state schools and their families. This case was broadened into a class-action lawsuit on behalf of all residents in three of the state schools. They argued that the conditions in the facilities violated various state and federal laws and the U. S. Constitution.

The out-of-court settlement reached in 1983 required the agency in charge to make a number of improvements. Two of those requirements are particularly worth noting.

The first, was an order to increase the number of trained staff at the schools so that the staff-to-patient ratio was higher. The second was a requirement that residents receive services in the least-restrictive setting possible. Translation: move more clients out of the state schools into smaller community-based residential care facilities. The results of these noble, new requirements were costly.

To comply, the mental health agency increased the staff-to-patient ratio by more than 50 percent and cut the number of patients in state schools from ten thousand down to sixty-seven hundred. But in doing so, costs went through the roof.

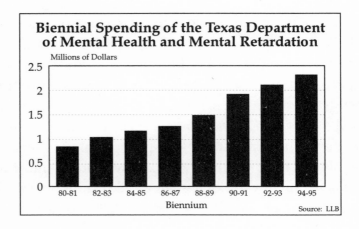

In order to maintain appropriate staff-to-patient ratios and reduce the number of patients, many of the state schools have been operating at a fraction of their full capacity. This has been extremely inefficient and costly. The state now spends over 50 percent more to care for most clients in state schools than it does to care for the same people in private sector facilities. Indeed, for one type of client, state school costs are now at more than $150 a day, compared to $94 a day in a private sector facility.

> **The state now spends over 50 percent more to care for most clients in state schools than it does to care for the same people in private sector facilities.**

Why not consolidate some of the clients into fewer schools and close the rest? The answer is politics and jobs, but more on that later. In a very modest first step, the Fort Worth State School is scheduled to be closed in 1995, and the Travis State School will shut down in 1999. In the meantime, hundreds of millions of dollars will be wasted due largely to court orders and political decisions made in response to court orders.

Where is Truck McGregor when we really need him?

## 84 Percent of the Budget

Entitlements, dedicated funds, and court orders—those are the primary driving forces behind the budget problems confronting our state. If you add them all up, they account for 84 percent of the entire state budget. That means that the legislature has total control of spending only 16 percent of the budget without changing state laws or the state constitution. Talk about being hogtied!

With 84 percent of the budget soaring ever higher, largely on autopilot, it is no wonder that state political leaders seem incapable of

> **With 84 percent of the budget soaring ever higher, largely on autopilot, it is no wonder that state political leaders seem incapable of controlling spending or addressing priorities. They continue to play the game by a set of rules that makes the state and the taxpayers big losers. It may not be Las Vegas, but here the dealer always wins.**

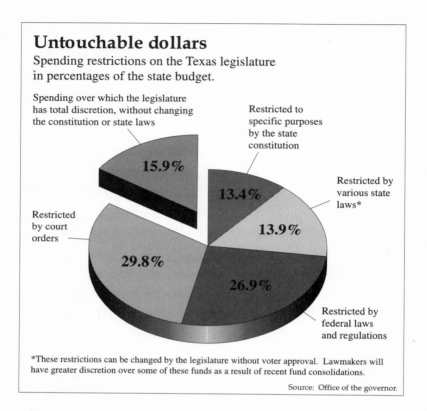

## Untouchable dollars

Spending restrictions on the Texas legislature
in percentages of the state budget.

Spending over which the legislature
has total discretion, without changing
the constitution or state laws

Restricted to
specific purposes
by the state
constitution

Restricted by
various state
laws*

15.9%

13.4%

13.9%

Restricted
by court
orders

29.8%

26.9%

Restricted by
federal laws
and regulations

*These restrictions can be changed by the legislature without voter approval. Lawmakers will
have greater discretion over some of these funds as a result of recent fund consolidations.

Source: Office of the governor.

controlling spending or addressing priorities. They continue to play the game by a set of rules that makes the state and the taxpayers big losers. It may not be Las Vegas, but here the dealer always wins.

And how have lawmakers chosen to pay the dealer? With a variety of taxes, the largest of which is the state sales tax. State politicians have also shifted a huge share of the burden to local authorities who have resorted regularly to increasing property taxes and augmenting the state sales tax. A quick look at the growth of both the sales and property taxes shows just how costly this uncontrolled spending has been, particularly in the last ten years.

The sales tax was first imposed in 1961 at a rate of 2 percent. It has been increased seven times, to its present level of 6.35 percent. Although originally somewhat limited, it has been broadened repeatedly to cover new transactions and services. Today cities, counties, hospital districts, and mass transit authorities all have the

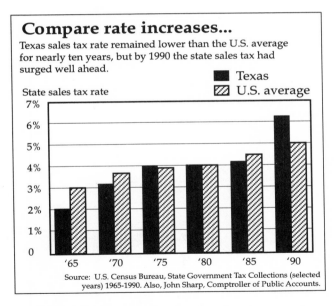

**Compare rate increases...**

Texas sales tax rate remained lower than the U.S. average for nearly ten years, but by 1990 the state sales tax had surged well ahead.

■ Texas
▨ U.S. average

State sales tax rate

Source: U.S. Census Bureau, State Government Tax Collections (selected years) 1965-1990. Also, John Sharp, Comptroller of Public Accounts.

authority to tack on additional sales taxes of up to 2 percent.

At the state level, the sales tax accounts for more than half of all revenues collected. Consequently, Texas has one of the highest sales tax rates in the country; the question is, how much higher can it go?

The same question can be asked about local property taxes. In 1981, local governments collected $5.7 billion in property taxes. Just a decade later, that had increased to $13.2 billion—a jump of 132 percent.

How much higher can it go? That will depend on whether we continue to do things the way they have always been done. What follows is a glimpse of future spending and tax increases sure to come. That is, if we do not change our ways. Brace yourself.

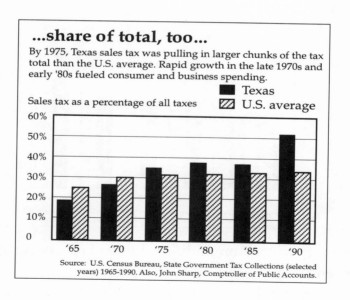

**...share of total, too...**

By 1975, Texas sales tax was pulling in larger chunks of the tax total than the U.S. average. Rapid growth in the late 1970s and early '80s fueled consumer and business spending.

Sales tax as a percentage of all taxes

■ Texas
▨ U.S. average

Source: U.S. Census Bureau, State Government Tax Collections (selected years) 1965-1990. Also, John Sharp, Comptroller of Public Accounts.

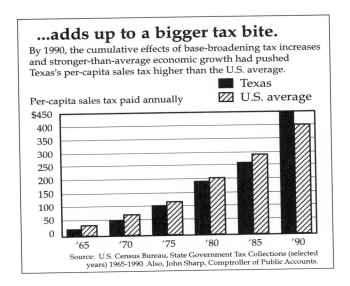

## ...adds up to a bigger tax bite.

By 1990, the cumulative effects of base-broadening tax increases and stronger-than-average economic growth had pushed Texas's per-capita sales tax higher than the U.S. average.

■ Texas
▨ U.S. average

Per-capita sales tax paid annually

Source: U.S. Census Bureau, State Government Tax Collections (selected years) 1965-1990. Also, John Sharp, Comptroller of Public Accounts.

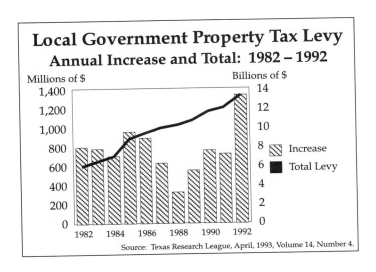

# Local Government Property Tax Levy
## Annual Increase and Total: 1982 – 1992

Millions of $

Billions of $

▨ Increase
■ Total Levy

Source: Texas Research League, April, 1993, Volume 14, Number 4.

27

# 2

# A Glimpse of the Future?
## $3 Trillion

Lyndon Johnson used to love to tell the story about an Army recruiter standing on a railroad platform back during World War II. The recruiter was about to send a green recruit off to basic training, when he decided that he would test the kid's intelligence.

"Son," he said, pointing down the track, "If you saw a train heading up this way at fifty miles an hour, and saw another train on the same track heading down this way at about the same speed, what would you do?"

The young soldier stood there for a second. He looked one way, and then the other. He scratched his head and said, "Well, sir, I guess I'd run and get my brother."

"Your brother? Why would you get your brother?" the recruiter asked.

" 'Cause my brother ain't never seen a train wreck before."

Well, that is precisely what is coming if we don't change our ways.

In 1947, the entire state budget was $319 million. It now stands at $35 billion. If spending continues to increase in the next forty-five years at the same pace it did the last, Texas will be burdened with a $3 trillion budget.

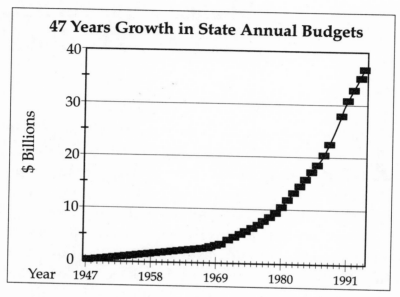

**47 Years Growth in State Annual Budgets**

Couple that with a recent book about the state's population growth entitled *Thirty Million Texans*, do some simple math, and here's what you get: If there are thirty million Texans forty-five years from now, every man, woman, and child will need to fork over $100,000 each year to support a budget exceeding $3 trillion.

Sound preposterous? No more so than a $35 billion-a-year budget would have sounded to folks back in 1948.

The current governor, lieutenant governor, and speaker of the house will point proudly to the budget passed in 1993 and claim that it was the first approved in years without a tax increase. (What they won't tell you is how they did it, or how likely—and some claim inevitable—a major tax increase will be in 1995 when the legislature meets again.) Because by then the 1994 election will be over, and Governor Richards and Lieutenant Governor Bullock hope they will have new, four-year contracts from the voters.

Now, it might be hard to believe, but elected officials do sometimes misrepresent things to voters. Take the Texas lottery, for example. Convinced by campaign rhetoric that the lottery would cure all that ails us, voters are rightfully dismayed today when they hear that even with the lottery revenue, more money is still needed for this program or that — especially education. In 1991, the *legislature* decided against dedicating all net lottery proceeds to education. It defeated a similar provision last session. But that's not the point. If every dime the state collects off the lottery for the next two years is pumped into public education, it would cover less than 7 percent of what is needed to keep the schools open.

> **I**f there are thirty million Texans forty-five years from now, every man, woman, and child will need to fork over $100,000 each year to support a budget exceeding $3 trillion.

Our state's leadership sold the lottery as the only alternative to a massive tax increase. The people bought it. In 1991, we got a lottery—and we got a $2.6 billion tax hike. We'll get another one next time the legislature meets.

The goal of the 1993 regular session of the legislature was very clear from the beginning—avoid a tax increase at all costs. Some will recall that Bullock proposed a state income tax in February 1991, just a month after taking office. He opposed the same tax in his campaign just four months before.

Apparently, the reaction he got to his income tax idea was so vehemently negative that he came to a startling conclusion: Texans are sick and tired of having their taxes increased. Because he was so impressed by this outpouring of public sentiment, Bullock has since led the charge in the legislature for a state constitutional amendment prohibiting an income tax without a vote of the people. Sounds like a man with religion, but what kind?

> **I**n any event, every bit of scotch tape, chewing gum, paper clips, and blue smoke and mirrors that could be found were employed in 1993 to postpone the next tax increase. Richards and Bullock have their re-election campaign ads already in the can: "We didn't raise your taxes."

In any event, every bit of scotch tape, chewing gum, paper clips, and blue smoke and mirrors that could be found were employed in 1993 to postpone the next tax increase. Richards and Bullock have their reelection

32

campaign ads already in the can: "We didn't raise your taxes."

*What they aren't telling you is that they have simply delayed state tax increases until after the next election by increasing your local property taxes now.* The difference here is the property tax hike will not have their names on it. A good question to ask candidates in 1994 is what do they plan to do in 1995 once the state has run out of budget gimmicks and accounting tricks to make ends meet. You will likely witness a shuffle that would make Muhammad Ali proud.

Why are higher state taxes so likely in 1995? One need only look at the last budget passed to see the storm clouds building over Austin. Let's start with public education.

The spending bill passed in 1993 appropriated $1.1 billion in extra funds for public education. While that is a hefty sum, it is probably $500 million short of what is required to keep up with just the growth in enrollment. Remember, public school districts are funded not by achievement or results but by the number of students in the classroom.

> **A** good question to ask candidates in 1994 is what do they plan to do in 1995 once the state has run out of budget gimmicks and accounting tricks to make ends meet. You will likely witness a shuffle that would make Muhammad Ali proud.

In addition to the $500 million shortfall for enrollment we already know about, there is still the question of funding equity which continues to linger. It will take almost $4 billion to "equalize" funding among rich and poor districts, and poor districts expect that money to come sometime in the future. The pressure to do more will persist.

## Criminal "Justice"

Another budget item that will escalate rapidly is criminal justice. Earlier, I mentioned criminal justice will become an entitlement in 1995. If that sounds strange, let me explain.

One of the many unfortunate aspects of the court orders affecting overcrowding in state prisons is that county jails have been forced to hold convicted inmates pending their transfer to state facilities. In other words, the problem of overcrowding is now shared with county jails, particularly in large, urban counties with serious crime problems.

In 1983, Texas's county jails had an average daily population of about eighteen thousand inmates. Ten years later, that figure had ballooned to more than fifty thousand. By 1992, more than one-third of all prisoners in county jails were convicted felons awaiting transfer to a state facility.

In fact, the county jails have been warehousing state prisoners for some time, which prompted them to file lawsuits to force the state to accept its prisoners. But because the state could not take these inmates fast

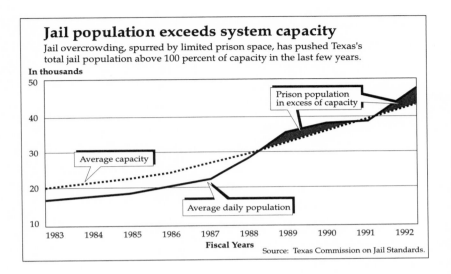

**Jail population exceeds system capacity**

Jail overcrowding, spurred by limited prison space, has pushed Texas's total jail population above 100 percent of capacity in the last few years.

In thousands

Prison population in excess of capacity

Average capacity

Average daily population

Fiscal Years

Source: Texas Commission on Jail Standards.

enough—the state prisons were full—the state, instead, decided to pay the counties to keep the felons. As part of legislation passed in 1991, the state agreed to pay counties either $20 or $30 per day, depending on a variety of factors, for every state prisoner in a county jail through 1995.

Harris County got a separate deal. As a result of a lawsuit filed in federal court, a judge ordered the state to pay a fine of $50 a day for every state inmate in the county jail over the court-established cap on jail populations. That fine went into effect in March 1993.

Starting in September 1995, the state has a duty to accept all felons in county jails within forty-five days after their paperwork is completed. To put it another way, counties are "entitled" to have state convicts accepted by a state institution. If that deadline is not met, another lawsuit will be triggered, and the state will be exposed to a huge financial liability with very poor grounds for a defense.

According to the Texas Criminal Justice Policy Council, there will be more than twenty-one thousand state prisoners backlogged in county jails by 1995, and some forty-six thousand by 2000. Counties will demand that the state pay for both housing and transportation of these inmates, and the cost to the state could easily exceed $250 million a year.

There will also be considerable costs associated with operating the thousands of new prison cells scheduled to come on line in the next few years. The annual payrolls for state prison employees alone are estimated to range from $3.5 million for each of ten small substance-abuse treatment facilities, up to $6 million for each of the four larger substance-abuse centers. And finally, the annual payroll for each of the maximum security units will be around $16 million. When those figures are added to the current prison operating budget, it's easy to see how criminal justice expenditures will explode in 1995 and beyond.

> The annual payroll for each of the maximum security units will be around $16 million. When those figures are added to the current prison operating budget, it's easy to see how criminal justice expenditures will explode in 1995 and beyond.

# A Glimpse of the Future? $3 Trillion

The high price tags on education and prisons in 1995 do not hold a candle to the incredible growth occurring in the health and human service area. That growth is driven primarily by the increased availability of Medicaid, the low-income health care program.

Remember that Medicaid is an entitlement program—all those who are poor enough to be served must be, regardless of the costs. However, unlike education and prisons, which are entitlements created by the state, Medicaid is a federal entitlement for which the state pays around 40 percent; the federal government pays the rest. As a result, federal officials set most of the rules.

Combined state and federal spending for Medicaid in Texas increased more than a billion dollars in 1992, and it will continue to spiral upward. In the appropriations bill passed in 1993, overall spending increased $7.2 billion. Of that increase, about 60 percent, or $4.3 billion, went to health and human services.

Why? Until five years ago, the primary means of becoming eligible for Medicaid was through welfare or Aid to Families with Dependent Children (AFDC). But in the 1980s, Congress passed changes in the Medicaid program enabling children and pregnant women who were poor, but not receiving welfare, to get Medicaid services. The results were dramatic.

Since 1987, the number of non-welfare Medicaid recipients has increased from a little more than thirty thousand to *five hundred thousand*.

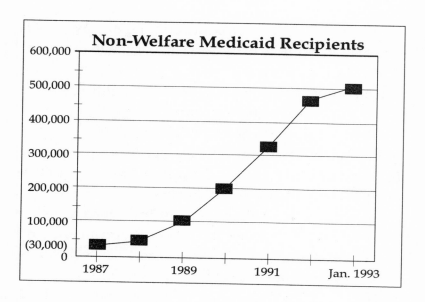

For the first time ever, the number of applicants for Medicaid actually has exceeded the number of applicants for welfare. This is all a result of changes in eligibility enacted by Congress. Given the Clinton administration's leanings on health care, it is difficult to imagine any reduction in the rate of increases that have occurred over the last five years. Instead, it is much more likely to get worse—from the standpoint of costs to the state—before it gets better.

## No Cost Control

Health and human services, which now account for 30 percent of the state's overall budget, could reach 50 percent before long. The sad truth is that Texas has very little control over those escalating costs. The state will just have to pay. This is why we must gain greater control over the parts of the budget that are within the legislature's jurisdiction.

One final component of the building budget storm is state employee benefits. Because public education, prisons, and health and human services—all of which are growing—are so labor-intensive, the cost of paying retirement, social security, and group insurance for the people who run these services has become a major budget item of its own. State-paid group insurance represents the largest area of increase. Collectively, employee benefits grew by more than $800 million between the 1990-91 budget and the 1992-93 budget. And they will increase by another $800 million by 1995, if fully funded. That brings the total cost for state

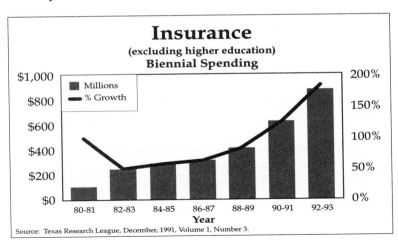

**Insurance**
**(excluding higher education)**
**Biennial Spending**

Source: Texas Research League, December, 1991, Volume 1, Number 3.

employee benefits to around $2.7 billion per year or $5.4 billion for the biennium.

If those figures do not provide a clear enough picture of the steady growth of state government over the next few years, maybe a snapshot of population trends in Texas will. Everyone knows how big Texas is, but few realize how fast Texas's population is growing compared to other states.

According to the 1990 census, Texas has become the third most-populous state in the nation, with roughly seventeen million people. But if present trends continue, Texas may well surpass New York to become the second-largest state by the year 2000. That is good for bragging rights, but the sheer number of people born or moving here will create a tremendous strain on state government.

The changing face of the Texas family could also spell trouble. In 1990, one-half of the households in this state consisted of one or two people. For the past several years, the traditional family—a married couple with children—has been decreasing. The nontraditional, new family is replacing it and tends to be poorer, particularly

> The nontraditional, new family is replacing it and tends to be poorer, particularly those families headed by women with young children. That helps explain why, contrary to popular mythology, Texas is not a wealthy state.

those families headed by women with young children. That helps explain why, contrary to popular mythology, Texas is not a wealthy state. Yes, many have made fortunes, but the average income in 1990 was $12,904 a year. That put Texas thirty-first among the fifty states and guarantees that the demand for government services will continue to grow rapidly in the years ahead.

For all these reasons, a glimpse at future state spending is extremely unsettling. While a $3 trillion budget may sound absurd, that is exactly what we will face—and pay for in taxes—in forty or fifty years, if we do not get control of government spending.

In the next chapter, I will examine carefully what we have to show for the billions of dollars we are spending. If you have read all you care to read about the problems, and want to cut to the solutions, skip the next chapter and pick up with chapter 4. Although it is helpful to have the background provided in "Where's The Beef" it is not a pretty picture. Parental discretion is advised.

# 3

# Where's the Beef?

everal years ago, a Wendy's television ad featured a spunky, elderly woman peering under the hamburger bun of a rival chain and yelling, "Where's the beef?"

The line struck a chord in people because it emphasized getting value for the dollar. It became the stuff of late-night monologues and even found its way into a presidential campaign.

In the years since that ad, Americans have focused increasingly on this question of value. The insistence on more value for the dollar forced U.S. automobile manufacturers to improve the quality of their cars or risk losing more of the market to foreign competitors. Value and quality are essential to the success of virtually

**So, why is it that at a time when we are increasingly insistent upon value and quality in the private sector, we are not equally demanding of government? Lord knows, it spends enough of our money.**

every business today, particularly manufacturing and service companies.

So, why is it that at a time when we are increasingly insistent upon value and quality in the private sector, we are not equally demanding of government? Lord knows, it spends enough of our money.

Why cannot we, as taxpayers, customers, consumers, and constituents, insist on value for the dollar we give to government? Haven't we earned the right to demand results for the billions and billions spent on government programs? Of course we have. And yet, the notion of accountability in government is a frightening prospect to most politicians and bureaucrats.

In the business world, accountability comes in the form of a balance sheet. If a business does not make a profit, it will eventually go broke. In government, there is no such bottom line. When a program fails to solve a problem, more often than not politicians decide to spend more money on it.

As a consequence, our elected officials have thrown billions of dollars at problems, hoping that alone would somehow improve the situation. They fail to realize that it is almost impossible to improve or manage what you cannot measure, and there are very few measurements of the effectiveness of government programs. Nowhere is that approach more apparent, nor a bigger disappointment, than in public education.

# Public Education

**B**etween 1980 and 1993, the number of students attending Texas public schools increased about 24 percent. But during the same time period, the amount of money spent on education increased more than 150 percent, going from $6.8 billion to more than $17 billion. Has the quality of education across the state improved proportionately? Has it improved at all?

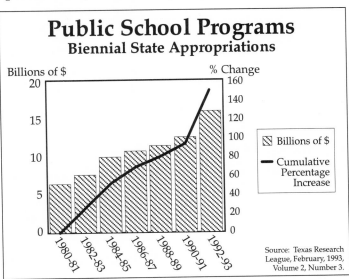

Even before concerns surfaced about the difference in test scores between American students and their counterparts overseas, even before the Texas legislature began its frustrating pursuit of equity in school finance, even before taxpayers began to protest the ever-increasing costs of education, there was growing uneasiness about the condition of education.

Seldom has one function of government been so ineffective. American students lag behind students in other countries in reading, science, and math. Too many drop out of school, and among those finishing, a substantial number lack the basic skills necessary to go to college or get a job. Mediocre test scores, problems with discipline, low teacher morale, spiraling costs, dissatisfied taxpayers, and frustrated elected officials are all part of the fabric of education in Texas.

**D**espite all these efforts, national SAT (Scholastic Aptitude Test) scores are about ninety points lower than their high thirty years ago. In Texas, recent SAT results showed only six states had lower math scores. Billions of dollars and repeated reforms have left our system of public education inefficient and ineffective.

Lack of effort is not the problem. In the last twenty years, the Texas Legislature has considered and passed plenty of "education reform" measures. In fact, so many attempts have been made at reform that it has begun to look like "*deja vu* all over again," as Yogi Berra used to say.

Despite all these efforts, national SAT (Scholastic Aptitude Test) scores are about ninety points lower than their high thirty years ago. In Texas, recent SAT results showed only six states had lower math scores. Billions of dollars and repeated reforms have left our system of public education inefficient and ineffective.

Regardless of the outcome of the ongoing debate over how to resolve the difference between the amount of money available to rich versus poor school districts, one thing is certain—the current education finance reform effort will not result in any significant improvement in student performance. Period.

Why can such a statement be made so flatly? Starting with the Coleman Report in 1966, 150 studies have shown no clear correlation or connection between spending on education and how much students learn. The five states (including the District of Columbia) with the highest SAT scores today do not spend the most money educating students. Iowa is number one, but ranks twenty-seventh in per-pupil expenditure. The others are North Dakota (forty-fourth in spending); South Dakota (forty-second); Utah (fifty-first, counting the District of Columbia) and Minnesota (twenty-fifth). And data from related sources suggest private church schools generally spend significantly less per student and yet have better results than public schools.

# Education as Business

Increasing the amount of funds that go to specific school districts might help improve some conditions and promote equity. However, improving the efficiency and effectiveness of our schools requires a fundamental change in the way we do business in education. As mentioned before, we fund schools based upon how many attend, without regard to how well those students are educated. David Kearns, former chairman of Xerox Corporation and deputy secretary of education in the Bush administration, said this about public education, "It is the only industry we have where if you do a good job, nothing good happens to you, and if you do a bad job, nothing bad happens to you."

The system of public education that has developed in Texas offers too few incentives to improve, much less achieve excellence. In fact, it mostly encourages mediocrity. One need only look at recent test scores to get the picture. This is not to suggest that the task of educating kids in the 1990s is an easy one. Changes in the family and ethnic mix have complicated matters enormously.

> **The system of public education that has developed in Texas offers too few incentives to improve, much less achieve excellence.**

However, pockets of excellence do exist in Texas schools. Sadly, those schools are more the exception than the rule. Take, for instance, Ysleta High School in El Paso. It is located in the middle of a barrio where unemployment is very high. Despite the fact that the school's facilities are old and battered, its students have consistently done well. Their scores on standardized tests compare favorably to some of the nation's most presti-

48

gious high schools, even though they lack the material advantages and have many students who must learn English as a second language. In fact, Ysleta made headlines in 1992 when five of its graduating seniors received substantial scholarships to attend the Massachusetts Institute of Technology.

Why is Ysleta succeeding when many other, better–funded schools are failing? What makes a school like Ysleta effective? Consider the research of John Chubb and Terry Moe, authors, professors, and nationally respected education experts:

"Decades of research on successful or effective schools identify several common characteristics. Effective schools have high expectations for students and teachers. They set rigorous academic standards, maintain order and discipline, require homework, and encourage parental support and cooperation. They have strong leadership from a principal, a stable staff of competent and enthusiastic teachers, a curriculum that is integrated across grade levels and that accommodates the variety of learning systems and cultural backgrounds of their students, and opportunities for parents to participate in their children's education. Underlying all of these elements is a set of clear and broadly accepted education goals—a vision or

> **D**oes this sound like pie in the sky or Alice in Wonderland education?  Perhaps it seems that way only in comparison to what we have today, which often looks more like Malice in Blunderland.

mission to which all members of the school community are committed."

Does this sound like pie in the sky or Alice in Wonderland education?  Perhaps it seems that way only in comparison to what we have today, which often looks more like Malice in Blunderland. Instead of giving principals and teachers the freedom to do what they do best, which is to educate children, the legislature has been more intent in recent years on telling the schools *how* to educate the kids. Some examples of recent state legislative mandates for school districts include

- the number of pupils per classroom
- the number of instructional hours per day
- the amount of in-service teacher training hours per year
- the number of essential elements to be taught per subject, and
- what kinds of essential elements are to be taught per subject

And yet, the same analysis by John Chubb and Terry Moe of some 150 different studies of school performance found no consistently positive and significant relationship between student achievement and many of the mandates imposed by our legislature.

What the legislature has *not* told teaching professionals is how to regain control of the classroom. Order and discipline in our schools is a serious problem and is making the task of educating kids much tougher both on the teachers and the students who want to learn.

Years ago, the three biggest disciplinary problems in the classroom were chewing gum, spitballs, and talking out of turn. No doubt there are many veteran educators who pine for those days of relative calm. Today, the problems include profanity, vandalism, theft, death threats, gang violence, and even murder. Obviously, the stakes today are much higher.

## "Ain't Behavin' "

In a survey taken by the Texas Federation of Teachers of more than fourteen hundred of its members across the state, 36 percent indicated that student discipline or misbehavior was a significant problem in their classroom. That figure was even higher in certain urban districts like the Houston Independent School District where 47 percent of teachers said discipline was a significant problem. Moreover, 85 percent said that discipline and misbehavior were significant problems outside the classroom in hallways or cafeterias.

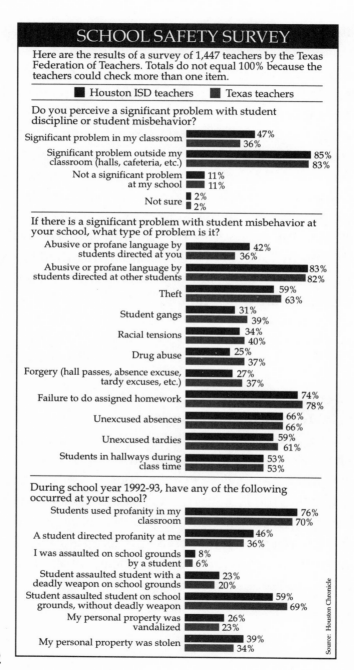

## SCHOOL SAFETY SURVEY

Here are the results of a survey of 1,447 teachers by the Texas Federation of Teachers. Totals do not equal 100% because the teachers could check more than one item.

■ Houston ISD teachers    ■ Texas teachers

**Do you perceive a significant problem with student discipline or student misbehavior?**

Significant problem in my classroom — 47% / 36%

Significant problem outside my classroom (halls, cafeteria, etc.) — 85% / 83%

Not a significant problem at my school — 11% / 11%

Not sure — 2% / 2%

**If there is a significant problem with student misbehavior at your school, what type of problem is it?**

Abusive or profane language by students directed at you — 42% / 36%

Abusive or profane language by students directed at other students — 83% / 82%

Theft — 59% / 63%

Student gangs — 31% / 39%

Racial tensions — 34% / 40%

Drug abuse — 25% / 37%

Forgery (hall passes, absence excuse, tardy excuses, etc.) — 27% / 37%

Failure to do assigned homework — 74% / 78%

Unexcused absences — 66% / 66%

Unexcused tardies — 59% / 61%

Students in hallways during class time — 53% / 53%

**During school year 1992-93, have any of the following occurred at your school?**

Students used profanity in my classroom — 76% / 70%

A student directed profanity at me — 46% / 36%

I was assaulted on school grounds by a student — 8% / 6%

Student assaulted student with a deadly weapon on school grounds — 23% / 20%

Student assaulted student on school grounds, without deadly weapon — 59% / 69%

My personal property was vandalized — 26% / 23%

My personal property was stolen — 39% / 34%

Source: Houston Chronicle

The biggest single problem identified by teachers was the use of abusive or profane language by students directed at other students. Failure to do assigned homework was the second biggest problem and unexcused absences was the third.

In Houston, more than 40 percent of the teachers said that students had directed abusive or profane language at them. The idea of a student getting away with something like that twenty years ago is completely foreign to most adult Texans, and yet it is a daily occurrence in many of our public schools. No wonder teacher morale is low in many areas, and burnout is a serious problem.

Much more will appear later about the breakdown or deterioration of the family, particularly as it relates to crime and welfare, but it has also had a dramatic impact on public education. As single-parent households become more commonplace, and extended-family child care less common, teachers increasingly are called upon to raise their students.

It is not surprising then that insufficient gains have been made in student performance in the last several years. Proof of that can be seen in the growing need for remedial training of high school graduates going on to college.

# Ill-Prepared

In 1992 more than 30 percent of Texas students entering college were not prepared academically to do so.

According to the Texas Academic Skills Program (TASP) exam given to high school graduates entering college, approximately one-third were in need of remedial training. Unfortunately, remedial training is neither quick nor cheap.

Of the group of first-year college students requiring remedial training in the 1989-90 academic year, some 38 percent had still not completed the needed catch-up work by April 1992, two and a half years later. That is one of the reasons why Texas has relatively low college graduation rates compared to other states' schools. A comparison from 1992 illustrates this point:

**Graduation Rates of Selected Texas Institutions:**

| | |
|---|---|
| Texas A&M University | 65% |
| University of Texas at Austin | 58% |
| Stephen F. Austin University | 39% |
| Texas Tech University | 38% |
| University of North Texas | 34% |
| Sam Houston State University | 32% |
| Southwest Texas State University | 28% |
| University of Texas at Arlington | 26% |
| University of Texas at El Paso | 26% |
| University of Texas at San Antonio | 19% |
| Lamar University | 18% |
| University of Texas at Pan American | 12% |

# Where's the Beef?

**Other States's Schools:**

| | |
|---|---|
| University of Michigan | 82% |
| University of Illinois (Urbana) | 78% |
| University of California at Berkeley | 73% |
| University of California at L.A. (UCLA) | 70% |
| University of California at Santa Barbara | 64% |

The financial cost to the state for remedial training is also very high. It now exceeds $125 million in the 1992-93 spending measure. Incredibly, Texas is spending $125 million in higher education to do what Texas public schools have already been paid to do, but failed.

Higher-education funding, unlike primary and secondary education, comes largely out of that 16 percent of the state budget that is not driven by entitlements, dedicated funds, or court orders. Consequently, it is all the more unfortunate that such a large part of those funds must be committed to finishing the job that should have been done by public high schools.

To make matters worse, the Texas legislature has begun a major expansion of funding for higher education in south Texas. While the notion of increasing educational opportunities for Hispanics in south Texas is commendable, the emphasis should be placed on strengthening primary and secondary school systems rather than adding more college-degree programs. The graduation rates for the University of Texas at San Antonio and University of Texas-Pan American are among the lowest in the state, and remedial training requirements are extremely high. Adding a new law school or medical school in south Texas is committing scarce resources to the wrong part of the educational process.

The ongoing need for remedial training, the lack of discipline and order, the disappointing results on standardized tests, and the constant increase in costs are evidence of a system in desperate need of change. They are also evidence of failure. Who is responsible for this failure? Where is the accountability?

> $W$e need a system that is based on achievements and results rather than just equity and enrollment.

The quality of public education in Texas will not improve until we stop rewarding failure. We need a system that is based on achievements and results rather than just equity and enrollment. It can be done, and I'll explain just how in the next chapter.

## Criminal Justice

If there is one place where the breakdown of the family has taken a costly toll both in terms of lives wasted and innocent people victimized, it is in the epidemic of crime sweeping our country. Barely a day passes that we are not shocked by some brutal act of random violence committed in one of our communities.

More often than not, the criminals have records dating back to their early teens.

Take the case of Marilyn Sage Meagher, a forty-three-year-old mother and real-estate agent living in Houston. She was found dead in her apartment with her throat cut on June 30, 1993. According to friends, she did not have an enemy in the world. But she did have a shiny new car that two teenagers wanted. They followed her home, killed her, and took her car. While it is shocking and tragic, it is all too commonplace.

One has to wonder what kind of societal conditions or circumstances could possibly produce such misguided youth. Is the family unit so fractured and damaged that these kids actually become teenagers without knowing basic right from wrong, or do they care? Perhaps the most disturbing aspect of the growth of crime is not only the absence of regard for other peoples' lives and property, but the frequent absence of remorse among those who are caught. For some, it is more like a game.

To those responsible for law enforcement, it is a constant struggle. In Texas the focus has been on locking up as many of the convicted criminals as possible. The frustration has been that

> **T**he frustration has been that only a fraction of the crimes committed are solved or reported; even those who are caught and convicted rarely serve the full sentence given them by a jury.

only a fraction of the crimes committed are solved or reported; even those who are caught and convicted rarely serve the full sentence given them by a jury. They are back out on the streets in no time preying on more innocent victims.

It is that pattern that has led to one of the most ambitious prison-building programs in the history of this nation. In 1992, Texas had approximately fifty-five thousand state prison beds. By 1995, that capacity will exceed 107,000. That is larger than most communities in Texas and represents an increase of more than 450 percent since 1980. The critical question is, will it make our lives, our homes, and our neighborhoods safer?

This state has spent billions of dollars already and is committed to spending billions more in a desperate attempt to provide greater security to its citizens without really knowing the answer to that question. Clearly, the alternative of releasing criminals due to overcrowding after they have served only a fraction of their time is unacceptable. Indeed, felons in state prison have been serving an average of only 13 percent of their sentences. State prison officials hope to increase that figure to 38 percent by the year 2000. But will that make our streets safer? Not much. Here is the problem.

## Crowded Prisons

Even with the huge increases in prison capacity scheduled to come on line by 1995, the Texas Criminal

Justice Policy Council estimates the prison population will grow even faster. They estimate that the backlog of state prisoners in county jails will increase from 19,000 to 21,000 by 1995 and to 46,000 by the year 2000. The total number of felons in the Texas criminal justice system will increase from 331,000 in 1993, to 388,000 by 1995, and 507,000 by the year 2000. Although that includes every state convict in prisons, jails, on parole or probation, it does not include some 200,000 misdemeanor offenders at the local level.

A second reason why the increased prison capacity might not provide the kind of protection we seek is that

> **E**ven with the huge increases in prison capacity scheduled to come on line by 1995, the Texas Criminal Justice Policy Council estimates the prison population will grow even faster.

a substantial portion of the predatory crimes are committed by juveniles or young adults. They are either too young to be tried as adults or unlikely to be sent to prison for their first felony conviction. And yet kids under the age of eighteen make up 25 percent of all people arrested and almost 50 percent of all those arrested for serious crimes.

The fact that many juveniles begin their careers in crime by the age of fourteen means they might not serve time in a state prison until they are in their twenties. Research indicates that once an individual embarks on a life of crime, those crimes increase until he or she reaches the age of twenty. From age twenty to age thirty, criminal activity decreases; after age thirty, a majority of criminal careers end. Therefore, the idea of serving time may not come into play until the criminal has begun to reduce his or her level of activity.

A third limitation on the effectiveness of incarceration is that it has become so commonplace among some communities that it has little or no deterrent effect. For instance, nearly half the youths in California's criminal justice training schools reported that a parent had also served time in prison. Moreover, some studies indicate that as many as 25 percent of inner-city males will be incarcerated in their lifetime.

Finally, another reason why more prisons alone may not reduce the amount of crime can be found in rearrest rates or recidivism. A Rand Corporation analysis recently studied two groups in California who committed similar crimes and had similar criminal records. The only difference between the two groups was the sentence given them. One group was sent to prison and the other group was placed on probation. After three years of tracking the groups, researchers found consistently higher rearrest or recidivism rates among the ones who went to prison than the ones placed on probation.

None of this is to suggest that prisons are not a critical component of the fight against crime. Any amount of time that a criminal spends behind bars is that much less time spent preying on others.

# Where's the Beef?

In the 1993 regular session of the legislature, a new penal code was enacted. This code is designed to establish clearer priorities for the imprisonment of different offenders. The most dangerous criminals will be required to serve at least half their sentence or thirty years, whichever is less, before they are eligible for parole. People who commit capital offenses, that is, crimes for which the death penalty is possible, must serve a minimum of forty years if they are not given the death penalty. That should help prevent the occurrence of another Kenneth McDuff incident.

McDuff was a Texas inmate who had been sentenced to death for murder. The sentence was overturned on a perceived technicality and he was mistakenly paroled. Once on parole, he committed another senseless murder and is now back in prison on death row.

His case created a public outcry and resulted in significant changes in parole procedures. Parole approval rates went from 81 percent in 1990 to less than 50 percent now. The new revised penal code goes a step further in reducing the flexibility of prison and parole officials over when certain dangerous criminals are released. It should help prevent the most violent offenders from repeating their crimes and put some teeth back into the sentences issued by juries. The question is, will it help prevent other violent criminals from simply taking their place?

Some observers of the national scene suggest that since the general population is aging, the crime rate should go down. This is based on the fact that juveniles are the age group most likely to commit crimes and since that group is shrinking in size, it should result in a reduction in the number of crimes they commit.

While that is true in most of the country, it is not true in Texas. Even though nationally, juveniles as a percentage of overall population fell by 7 percent between 1981 and 1991, it rose by 16 percent in Texas. As a consequence, Texas juvenile crime is going up, and violent crimes by juveniles are rising even more rapidly.

Juvenile arrests in Texas increased by 34 percent from 1981 to 1991 while those across the nation fell by nearly 12 percent. Arrests for violent crimes by juveniles went up 98 percent in Texas during the 1980s, while the national increase was up a meager 8 percent. In other words, Texas juveniles are committing an increasingly high percentage of the violent crimes in our state.

What types of crimes are they committing? The following figures represent a five year referral pattern from the Texas Juvenile Probation Commission:

| Type of Crime | Percent Increase |
| --- | --- |
| Felony Drug Arrests | 287% |
| Homicides | 143% |
| Violent Delinquent Acts | 122% |
| Juvenile Weapons Convictions | 95% |
| Delinquent Acts | 55% |

Less than 3 percent of the juveniles perpetrating these crimes are actually committed to a Texas Youth Commission facility, and those are the most serious and chronic juvenile delinquents. Of those committed, 46 percent had multiple felony adjudications and 31 percent had five or more felony referrals.

In short, the juvenile justice system is totally overwhelmed and ill-equipped to handle the alarming increase in juvenile crime in the last ten years. Building more prisons for adults is helpful, but it will not measurably reduce the crime rate until we come to grips with the juvenile problem in Texas.

The fact is that a frightening number of kids in Texas are growing up in households in which values and morality are absent. They have little or no regard for the lives or property of others and seem to view the law-enforcement process with disdain. That must change.

At the rate things are going, spending on criminal justice in Texas is doubling every five years. Shouldn't we be getting more in the way of protection and safety for the dollars invested?

> **At the rate things are going, spending on criminal justice in Texas is doubling every five years.**

While the focus has been on locking up as many criminals as can be caught and convicted, we have largely ignored the principal spawning ground for future criminals: juveniles. Moreover, the state is doing next to nothing to increase the likelihood that criminals will get a job when they are out of prison.

Is this the best we can do? By 1995, Texas will have more prison cells and will be spending more on criminal justice than many countries in the world. Where is the accountability in the system? Even if prison space is used effectively, Texas faces a monumental obstacle to developing a coherent and successful criminal justice strategy. The present criminal justice system divides responsibility and control between the state and literally hundreds of jurisdictions. The resulting process is a management nightmare.

The number of people coming into the state prison system is controlled by local authorities. They are responsible for apprehending, trying, and sentencing criminals. They have no control over the rehabilitation or lack thereof of these offenders, or even how much of the sentence given will actually be served. Yet, most of the offenders sent to prison will return to those local communities after they are released.

State officials, on the other hand, while responsible for the operations and expense of the prison system, have no direct control over how many people are sent to prison. Early release or parole procedures are the only means the state has of managing the size of the prison population. Those procedures have succeeded in making a mockery of the entire criminal justice system.

State officials control part of that system, local officials control part, but neither controls all of it. As a result, when something goes wrong, everyone points fingers at everyone else.

Any effective attack on crime must deal with this division of control and responsibility. It must also deal with the absence of any solutions to the juvenile problems facing us and the lack of rehabilitation. In other words, we need a criminal justice strategy that will make criminals pay for their crimes, but try to break the patterns that now exist. Some specific proposals in that regard will be outlined in the next chapter.

## Health and Human Services

The two largest programs in the health and human services area are Medicaid and welfare. As I previously pointed out, Medicaid is the low-income, health-care program that's grown dramatically in the past few years. That growth is a direct result of changes in eligibility rules enacted by the Congress in the late 1980s and imposed upon the states.

While states may attempt to control the increasing costs of Medicaid, their flexibility to do so is limited by another congressional mandate which prohibits states from cutting funding to Medicaid because of their own budget problems. It is the classic Catch-22. Why else would a state try to restrain cost increases for Medicaid if it were not for the purpose of controlling its own budget? As a consequence, Medicaid costs are destined to continue through the roof and there is very little individual states can do to prevent it.

Welfare, or Aid to Families with Dependent Children (AFDC) as it is known in Washington, D.C., was established as part of the Social Security Act of 1935. It is a cash-benefit program originally intended to provide a safety net for those with dependent children who are unable to work. In the past thirty years, it has ripened into a way of life for millions of Americans and has had an incredibly destructive impact on the family.

Texans have always had a strong work ethic and a deep suspicion of government "giveaway" programs. So, welfare has never been a particularly popular program here. To the extent that the state could control it, Texas has sought consistently to make welfare payments so low that no poor person in his or her right mind would move to Texas to get welfare.

However, welfare is a joint federal-state program. That means that the federal government pays approximately 60 percent of the cost and the state pays the balance. It also means that the federal government in general, and the U.S. Congress in particular, set many of the rules for who becomes eligible to receive welfare. It is those rules that have been such an unmitigated disaster.

Instead of welfare serving as a temporary safety net for those who are disadvantaged or down and out, it has become a vicious trap from which it is extremely difficult to escape. It encourages and rewards all the wrong types of behavior and discourages or punishes all the right types.

For instance, until recently if a man and woman were happily married with a dependent child, but were dirt poor, they would not qualify for welfare because the husband was at home. But if the husband abandoned the family, the wife and her children could qualify. That was the rule in twenty-three states, including Texas, until five years ago. It will take decades to overcome the destructive impact of that rule on millions of poor families.

Second, a program that should encourage people to escape welfare by rewarding work does just the opposite. Until recently, if a welfare recipient took a full-time minimum wage job in Texas, he or she lost most of his or her benefits immediately. Those benefits included not only welfare, but also Medicaid for which a person automatically qualifies when on welfare. When they added it all up, most recipients found themselves doing better on welfare with benefits like health care than they were in a minimum wage job in the private sector. Is it any wonder that millions of

> **W**hen they added it all up, most recipients found themselves doing better on welfare with benefits like health care than they were in a minimum wage job in the private sector. Is it any wonder that millions of mothers with dependent children chose welfare over work?

67

mothers with dependent children chose welfare over work? They did better doing nothing than going out and getting a job!

It was not until 1988 that Congress passed legislation requiring all states to cover two-parent households that were poor enough for welfare. And it was not until that same legislation in 1988 that Congress attempted to phase out welfare benefits in a way that rewards the people who go to work rather than punishing them. In the meantime, there are second and third generations of families that have lived off welfare and have no idea what it is like to have a permanent job. Although all able-bodied welfare recipients have been required for years "to look for work" while receiving welfare, that requirement has not been enforced effectively and, thus, has become something of a joke.

For more than twenty-five years, this country has suffered through failed welfare policies. They were destined to fail because funding was based more upon how many people the welfare bureaucracy could add to the rolls as eligible than how many people were moved off the rolls into permanent jobs. This is another case of a government program in which there were no standards for measuring effectiveness or success.

In the absence of such standards, a huge welfare bureaucracy has developed for the single purpose of supporting and, some would say, perpetuating a dependent class of welfare recipients. In order to fully appreciate the size and scope of the problem in Texas, one needs to get a picture of the average welfare family in our state.

That family consists of a single mother with two children. Approximately 40 percent of the families are African-American, 40 percent are Hispanic, and 20 percent are white. In order to qualify for welfare in Texas, one must be extremely poor with virtually no personal property of value, including a car.

Once a family qualifies, it will receive no more than $184 per month in cash benefits. In addition to the cash, it will receive about $300 worth of food stamps and will be covered under Medicaid.

Some families have been on welfare for generations. Others enter and exit the welfare rolls repeatedly. Indeed, about one-third of those on welfare have been on the rolls for one year or less. About another 40 percent have been on the rolls for less than four years, and about another 30 percent have been on the welfare rolls for over four years. The welfare population in Texas is not the sort of static mass that some would expect. However, once a family has been on welfare, it finds it very difficult to escape it for long.

The welfare population in Texas tends to be poorer than the national average and has very limited job skills. Indeed, the vast majority of welfare mothers read at about a fourth-grade level. They have very little personal confidence or self-esteem and are intimidated by the welfare bureaucracy they must deal with.

I served as a volunteer on the board of the Texas Department of Human Services, the state welfare agency, from 1987 through 1990. In my four years on the board, I came to the conclusion that most welfare recipients do not want to be on welfare but find it impossible to escape. Among many, there is a sense of resignation that the cards are stacked against them and that they will never get a break. In fact, the more one learns about the welfare bureaucracy and the red tape, the easier it is to understand why so few recipients escape the rolls for long.

> **M**ost welfare recipients do not want to be on welfare but find it impossible to escape. Among many, there is a sense of resignation that the cards are stacked against them and that they will never get a break.

In addition to serving on the board of the Texas Department of Human Services, I also served on the State Job Training Coordinating Council. The council is charged with overseeing the expenditure of more than $230 million annually of federal money to provide job training for people who are "economically disadvantaged." That is another Washington, D.C. term for "poor."

Clearly, folks on welfare—particularly in Texas—are economically disadvantaged. Indeed, if one is poor enough to qualify for welfare in Texas, they are definitely poor enough to qualify for job training under this federal program known as the Job Training Partnership

Act (JTPA). So I asked the question, if you are poor enough to qualify for welfare and therefore, plenty poor enough to qualify for JTPA, does that mean that welfare recipients automatically qualify for job training under this federal program? The answer was no. In fact, if a welfare recipient seeks job training, they had to fill out a whole new set of forms and prove, again, that they were poor enough to qualify. What a ridiculous requirement and an incredible waste of time!

It seems that the bureaucrats who run the job training program are not the same as the ones who run welfare. Even though both bureaucracies are supposed to be serving many of the same people, expecting bureaucrats in different agencies to work well together is expecting the abnormal. In fact, cooperation of that sort was once described to me as an unnatural act between nonconsenting adults.

Because I had responsibilities involving both welfare and job training, I led the charge for establishing automatic job-training eligibility for welfare recipients. In other words, once someone proved he was poor enough for welfare, he did not have to prove the same thing again to different bureaucrats to qualify for job training. After all, the goal is to get people off welfare and into permanent jobs, not to erect as many bureaucratic barriers as possible and strangle them in red tape. Not only did I want one eligibility screening instead of two, but I wanted a one-page form to prove that eligibility.

It took two years and the eventual signing of an executive order by then-Governor Bill Clements, but we got it done. A very simple, common-sense idea to make it easier for welfare recipients to do the right thing, get job training, and get off welfare took two years. It makes you wonder whose side the bureaucrats are on.

Theresa Funiciello has no doubt about the answer to that. As a former welfare recipient and then welfare worker in New York, she describes the welfare bureaucracy and the nonprofit service sector that supports it as "poverty pimps."

Funiciello's *The Tyranny of Kindness* offers a stinging indictment of the entire system. "The welfare state is not new to the late-twentieth century, but the non-profit service sector has never been richer (in terms of share of the gross national product and jobs), more powerful or less accountable. . . . It has become a veritable fifth estate. Taxpayers foot the bill. Poor people suffer the consequences."

She claims the "poverty pimps" have no monetary incentive to help people get off welfare. In fact, the more people on welfare, the more secure their function. Based upon my experience, there is a great deal of truth to her arguments. While many in the welfare bureaucracy in Texas are committed to helping people, others are merely committed to keeping their jobs.

If a decision comes down to choosing between what is best for the taxpayer or recipient versus what is best for the department, the department usually wins out.

The survival and well-being of its staff has become more important than the survival and well-being of those it was created to serve. That may be human nature, but it does not have to be acceptable at the state welfare department or any other agency in Austin.

## Improve Accountability

As mentioned previously, most of the welfare programs are under federal control. However, that does not mean that Texas is incapable of doing things better. We must establish much greater accountability for those who make up the welfare bureaucracy and seek federal permission, or waivers, to try new approaches to ending welfare as an acceptable way of life. Those approaches must reward productivity and initiative rather than idleness and dependence.

Too many tax dollars have already been wasted and too many productive lives lost to continue what we are doing. Whether the subject is public education, criminal justice, or health and human services, it is high time we started doing things differently. It is time we started paying for performance rather than rewarding failure. That is the focus of the next chapter.

# Part II:

# Doing Things Differently

# 4

# Getting Our
# ABCs in Order

Any book about Texas must mention Sam Houston at least twice. So, here's another of my favorite stories about the father of our great state.

Texas won its independence from Mexico at the Battle of San Jacinto on April 21, 1836. Houston led a ragtag bunch of soldiers and volunteers to victory over the superior forces of Mexican President Santa Anna late that afternoon. It was no conventional battle.

Realizing his Texas forces were no match for the larger, better-trained Mexican Army, Houston had to be resourceful. He had to fight smarter. Over the grumbling of his men, Houston delayed the battle until his weary enemy was deep into its daily siesta. He also ordered a critical escape route for his own men—Vince's Bridge spanning the Buffalo Bayou—destroyed. "It cut off all means of escape for either army," Houston later said. "There was no alternative but victory or death."

Unconventional tactics gave Texas one of its greatest moments. That victory not only helped avenge the loss of General William Barret Travis and his brave men at the Alamo, but it also sent a clear signal to the leadership of the young United States. It exemplified the sort of strength, courage, independence, and resourcefulness for which this state has become known. It made Texas different.

In the years since we joined the Union, Texas has produced more than its share of leaders and leadership.

As we approach the end of the twentieth century, Texans have a new opportunity to prove that we can do things better. We have an opportunity to show that state government can work better without constantly increasing spending and raising taxes. And we have a chance to lead this country in creativity and innovation. But first, we must come to grips with our immediate problems and declare that the status quo is unacceptable.

Pulitzer Prize-winning historian and author Daniel J. Boorstin said, "The greatest obstacle to progress is not ignorance, but the illusion of knowledge." The current leadership of our state is wedded to the assumption that we have run out of options. They figure that in order to keep up with the skyrocketing cost of state government, either services must be cut drastically, or taxes must be raised again.

The third option that few in Austin seem to be able or willing to consider is changing the assumptions upon which we base government and mustering the courage to do things differently.

The "same-old same-old" is simply not getting the job done. Our present public school system is costing more, but producing less. Our criminal-justice system is becoming a black hole for cash without measurably increasing public safety. And our health and human services safety net is swelling so fast it may collapse of its own weight.

If Texas is to be a leader rather than a follower in an increasingly competitive national and international economy, it must have a work force that is highly motivated, well-educated, and adequately trained. It cannot afford a government that consumes more and more of the fruits of our labor and delivers less and less. And it cannot afford a society in which the working men and women are supporting an ever-expanding class of unproductive and idle human beings.

> **The current leadership of our state is wedded to the assumption that we have run out of options. They figure that in order to keep up with the skyrocketing cost of state government, either services must be cut drastically, or taxes must be raised again.**

That means we must spend existing tax revenues smarter and more creatively and find new ways of prompting individual responsibility instead of debilitating dependence. We can start by identifying a basic set of principles that will guide our new approach.

1.   Reward success instead of failure. Base budgeting on results achieved.

2. Seek free-market solutions that will create competition and increase efficiency.
3. Push decision-making as close to the people or customers as possible.

By applying these principles, we can begin to establish accountability for the billions of tax dollars yet to be spent. Also, we can see that the needs of our citizens will be met, not the needs of those providing the service.

While there are some in state government now talking about linking budget appropriations to "outputs," such as educational achievement, rather than "inputs," such as numbers of students enrolled, it is more rhetorical than real. As long as the vested interests in Austin remain firmly in control of the process, paying for performance will not happen. They cannot stand the accountability.

# Headed toward Decadence

There is another aspect of doing things differently which must be addressed here. It does not fit neatly under the heading of how to make state government work better. Rather, it relates to one of the most serious problems facing our nation, and facing our state. That problem is what former Drug Czar William J. Bennett describes as "cultural decadence, moral disorientation, and a fraying social fabric."

# Getting Our ABCs in Order

Despite a widespread desire, particularly among many in the "baby-boomer" generation, not to be "judgmental," or to focus on issues of morality, we must. The breakdown of the family and the resulting absence of values and character among many of our children is an integral part of the social problems we face.

Whether the subject be high school dropouts, juvenile delinquency, teenage pregnancy, or drug dependency, a dominant factor is that families are not functioning in any traditional sense. They are families in which character, virtue, and any belief in a higher power are either not taught to or not accepted by the children. The rock or rap singer, the gang leader, and the television set are more prevalent influences. The result is children without a moral compass, little self-esteem, and few positive role models.

We all know government cannot instill values or build self-esteem. It can, however, contribute to their destruction, such as in the case of welfare policies that encourage fathers to abandon their wives and children.

Only individuals—through their families, churches, synagogues, and other institutions—can help reestablish character, virtue, and morality as underlying precepts for our society and state. We simply cannot expect the government to do it for us.

In the proposals that follow, I will try to apply the three principles of basing funding on results, creating competition, and forcing decision making as close to the customer as possible. However, there is also a recognition that a large part of the solution to our problems rests not with government but with individual action and responsibility.

## Public Education: Creating a System Second-to-None

The problems facing public education in Texas today have been well documented. They include disappointing test scores, a lack of discipline and order, low teacher morale, centralized control, and soaring costs. All too often, falling test scores have been used as a justification for increased spending.

In recent years, the debate has centered around the elusive pursuit of equity in funding between rich and poor school districts. But the truth is that spending on public education has increased by more than 150 percent since 1980, and the state has very little to show for it.

Public education has long been a top priority of this state, and it will continue to be so. That is the good news. But then we have to ask why, given the priority in funding public education, is there such a huge gap between the dollars invested and the quality of education received by Texas children? There are three reasons.

*First, funding is not based on results.* Public education is an entitlement program which is driven by student enrollment and a host of other factors which bear little relation to educational achievement. The more students who attend a school, the more state aid that school receives, regardless of what kind of job it is doing. Instead of paying for performance, we are often rewarding failure.

*Second, there is little or no competition among schools for students.* Most folks have no alternative, but to send their child to a public school in their neighborhood. As a consequence, education consumers cannot take their business elsewhere if they are unhappy with the product or service. The lack of options notwithstanding, frustration with the failings of our public education system have still forced many parents to pursue alternative schools, or to provide home schooling.

*Third, most of the major decision making is centralized in the hands of the legislature, education agency bureaucrats, or district school officials.* The principals, teachers, and parents simply do not have the authority to devise education plans which are best suited to their kids. Recently, education leaders have begun to move toward "site-based management" of schools, but that movement comes very late and, for many, very reluctantly.

What we need is a new system with a new set of rewards and incentives. That system should base funding increases on results. Local schools should be given the flexibility and authority to develop their own education plans, within limits set by the state. And finally, parents should be given the right to choose the school their child will attend. Let me explain.

The American economy is built on rewarding performance. If a business can provide a quality product or service at a competitive price, it is usually rewarded by making a profit. While schools are not in the business of making a profit, they are in the business of teaching our kids. Given the investment of so many dollars by so many taxpayers, we have the right to expect a higher quality product than what we're getting today.

To reward the pursuit of academic excellence and administrative efficiency, funding increases should be tied to improvements in performance of individual schools. Each school would retain a base level of funding that reflects current enrollment. Funding beyond that level would depend on performance.

The legislature should provide the means by which improvements in performance could be measured, and then give individual schools the power to formulate their own strategy for getting there. Schools that are already performing well or are well-funded, would not be eligible for as much additional support as schools that have low performance and have ample room for improvement. In other words, schools that are currently not performing well have the most to gain from such an approach.

Schools that are already performing well should be rewarded with greater autonomy and freedom from state and district control. I like the concept of "charter schools." A charter school is a semi-autonomous public school established by a contract negotiated with either a local school board or a state board of education. A half-dozen states are experimenting with the concept that allows public schools to be custom-designed by teachers and parents to meet specific educational needs. In Colorado, for example, a charter school is subject to all federal and state laws. It must be open to all children within a district, must be non-religious, and cannot have previously operated as a private school.

But it can negotiate for freedom from some school district policies and state regulations. It must, however, show that it gets results equal to or better than regular schools. Money follows the students. The exact amount is subject to negotiations with a board.

Over the last three years in Texas, school-based committees of parents, teachers, and principals have been organized. Although their discussions have moved far beyond the previous focus on bake sales and school carnivals, these committees have not given parents the role in decision making that they expected. For instance, parents very appropriately want to participate in the continuation or selection of their school principals, and are disappointed to find that the choice is usually made by "higher-ups" who did not bother to consult them.

> **To reward the pursuit of academic excellence and administrative efficiency, funding increases should be tied to improvements in performance of individual schools. Each school would retain a base level of funding that reflects current enrollment. Funding beyond that level would depend on performance.**

Several such incidents occurred within the Houston Independent School District at Lamar, Scarborough, and Bellaire high schools. As one Bellaire High School parent put it, "I don't understand why it takes so long to move a big bureaucracy in a new direction. Parents don't feel they have any power at all. They feel overwhelmed and powerless and frustrated." The reason for that frustration is that most education bureaucrats are not really committed to sharing decision making power.

As researchers John Chubb and Terry Moe have said, there are many steps which local schools might take to improve performance. They include

1. setting rigorous academic standards
2. maintaining order and discipline
3. requiring homework
4. establishing a staff of competent and enthusiastic teachers, and
5. encouraging parental support and participation

## Raising Educational Expectations

One of the most important ingredients to improving performance is raising the expectations of the students, teachers, and parents about what can be accomplished. If expectations are low, performance will remain low. However, if expectations are high, performance will often rise to those expectations, regardless of other obstacles.

While regular testing of students must be an integral part of the performance measures developed by the legislature, credit should also be earned for progress on many of the specific steps listed above. We do not want to create a system in which too much funding rides on a single test. That only encourages schools to teach the kids how to take a particular test and distracts teachers from expanding their broader education.

An essential element of schools earning more funding for their improved performance is giving them the discretion to spend that additional funding as they see fit. That does not mean authorizing them to offer belly dancing classes, but rather allowing them to pay their teachers more or deal with a variety of other conventional needs.

The flexibility at the school level should be a real incentive for principals and teachers to strive for improved results, but there is another step that should be taken on the road to education excellence. That step is to offer parents choices regarding where they send their children to school and to create real competition between schools for the education dollar.

Public education in America is largely a monopoly and as Peter Drucker, the great management expert, said, that makes this nation "the only major developed country in which there is no competition within the school system." Clearly, we are not talking about athletic competition, but competition for consumers—parents and their kids.

# Deep in the Heart

John Norquist, the Democratic Mayor of Milwaukee where school choice has become a reality, wrote the following in a July 1993 issue of *Reader's Digest*:

"Like many revolutionary ideas, school choice is rooted in common sense. Most of us see each day how competition spurs achievement— whether in playing baseball, selling soft drinks, building computers or discovering cancer drugs. Choice drives the same spur into the haunches of the public-school monopoly.

"Protected against competition, the public-school bureaucracy serves itself, not students, and with predictable results. Our children have little prospect for improvement because our schools pay no penalty for failure. In fact, we reward failure. Every sign of declining student performance becomes just one more reason to increase funding."

Exactly what is school choice? Simply stated, it enables parents to direct funds to the school that they think will do the best job of educating their child. The education dollars follow the student rather than the student following the dollars. That competition for students is what improves efficiency and performance.

How would it work in Texas? Each public school student would be given a voucher which could be presented at any school, subject only to space available and ethnic mix. That voucher would be like a check from the state.

A system of true choice would permit the use of vouchers at private as well as public schools. However, such changes must be implemented gradually. The first step would be to establish choice among public schools, and then follow with private schools willing to participate. If, in the face of performance-based funding and competition, certain schools cannot make the grade, they should be placed on probation. If they still fail to improve their performance, they should be shut down.

> **A**ny system of true choice would permit the use of vouchers at private as well as public schools.

Conventional wisdom would have us believe that poor schools, inner-city schools, or schools with high minority student bodies would be hurt if they are forced to compete or perform to obtain funding. That conventional wisdom has been proven wrong. In their book, *Reinventing Government* (1992), David Osborne and Ted Gaebler cite the case of one of the nation's poorest school districts, located in East Harlem, New York:

"The results of District 4's experiment (with school choice) has been startling. Reading scores are up sharply: In 1973, 15 percent of junior high students read at their grade level;

by 1988, 64 percent did. Writing skills have improved: in 1988, state tests found that 75 percent of the district's eighth-graders were competent writers. And the percentage of District 4 graduates accepted to New York's four elite public high schools, such as Bronx Science and Brooklyn Technical, has shot up. In the mid-1970s, fewer than ten of District 4's graduates were admitted to these schools each year. By 1987, 139 were—10 percent of District 4's graduates, almost double the rate for the rest of New York City. Another 180 attended a second tier of selective public high schools. And thirty-six went to selective private schools, including Andover and The Hill School. All told, more than a quarter of District 4's graduates earned places in outstanding high schools—schools that were virtually off limits fifteen years before."

Another inspiring example of school choice that has successfully challenged the assumed limitations of a predominantly minority student body is Messmer High School in Milwaukee. This school is located in the inner city with 70 percent of its students minority.

The Catholic Diocese quit supporting it in the mid-1980s. In debt, lacking adequate equipment and facilities, and facing changing demands, it looked like it might be closed for good.

But Brother Bob Smith, its principal, reopened Messmer as a private school without church support. It is based on a philosophy of accountability, small classes, and parent involvement, all concepts that were more common in public schools in the 1950s and 1960s.

Messmer also teaches values. "There is nothing wrong with talking about morals and ethics in school," Smith says. "The fact that we're not teaching values in our public schools really is teaching a set of values by telling kids this is a society without values."

Parents must participate by attending three parent-teacher conferences each year. If the parents don't show up, the children cannot attend class the next day. If that were not unconventional enough, student performance and responsibility is rewarded in a meaningful way. Students with A or B averages are allowed to leave school every day after the eighth period. Others must stay and receive additional instruction.

> **S**tudents with A or B averages are allowed to leave school every day after the eighth period. Others must stay and receive additional instruction.

Some might argue with Brother Bob's approach, but no one can question his success. On the average, 96 percent of his students attend school each day. Messmer graduates 98 percent of its students within four years, and 78 percent go on to college. In short, Messmer is succeeding as the school of choice for some of the most economically disadvantaged kids you could ever find.

Another example of school choice recently launched in Texas is the Children's Educational Opportunity Foundation (CEO) program in San Antonio. The purpose of the CEO Foundation is to assist in equalizing opportunities for low-income children in the San Antonio area by providing tuition vouchers up to $750 per year. That works out to be roughly half the cost of tuition at the participating private schools. Every dime used to pay for the vouchers has come from private donations.

Kids are provided vouchers on a first-come, first-served basis and the commitment is for a period of three years. Since its inception in April 1992, the group has processed more than twenty-six hundred applications, assisted 930 students, and has seventy-three separate schools participating.

This is the brainchild of Dr. James R. Leininger, the founder of a medical supply company named Kinetic Concepts, Inc. He wanted to provide low-income families of San Antonio the same opportunity to send their children to private schools that wealthier families enjoy. Under Leininger's leadership, the CEO Foundation has raised well over $1.5 million, and has inspired the creation of a similar program in Austin. While the Austin program will begin on a much smaller scale, it will be aimed at the same low-income families—those who already qualify for the federal free-lunch program.

What does it mean to a family or child to have the choice of attending a public or private school? For Etta Wallace, it means giving her three teenage boys not just a chance to learn, but to survive.

"The biggest thing is I want my kids to be safe. I don't want to have to worry about them getting jumped by the gangs. That's what was happening at the public school," she said, sitting on the concrete front porch of her modest home on the east side of San Antonio. "But the gangs were just part of it. I felt like the teachers weren't doing their job, or the principals either."

Thanks to the CEO Foundation program, Bobby, sixteen, and his twin brothers, Terry and Tony, thirteen, were enrolled in private Catholic schools in 1992. But it has not been easy for the Wallace family. "There have been times when I had to let the light bill go to pay for the tuition for my kids," said Etta, a single mother. "But at least I have a choice about where I spend my money."

The family does not own a car so the boys must travel by public transportation to their school six miles away. They wake up at 5:00 A.M., take a bus downtown, transfer to another bus, and arrive at their school just before 8:30 A.M.

"When Mom said she was sending us there, I said no way," explained Bobby. "Now, after being there, I told her there's no way I'm going back to public school. Now, I don't have to worry about the gangs beating up my brothers."

It is not surprising that some of the strongest support for school choice now comes from African-American and Hispanic lawmakers, who believe the public school system has failed to adequately prepare minority students for either college or the workplace.

Texas State Representative Ron Wilson, an African-American Democrat from Houston, represents constituents who are predominantly minority and low-income. As he put it, "I've stuck with the current public-education system for the sixteen years I've been in office. I still have many children graduating who are functionally illiterate. Public schools should either educate the children or set them free." In other words, let them pursue alternatives.

> **I**t is not surprising that some of the strongest support for school choice now comes from African-American and Hispanic lawmakers, who believe the public school system has failed to adequately prepare minority students for either college or the work place.

A similar frustration prompted State Representative Henry Cuellar, a Democrat from Laredo, to offer his own voucher program for economically disadvantaged kids. He proposed a pilot project in fourteen of the one thousand-plus school districts around the state.

"My district is 94-percent Hispanic and has a very high poverty level," said Cuellar. "Why shouldn't a child from a poor family have an opportunity to attend a private school?" It would certainly put the debate over equity in an entirely different light. What could be more equitable than giving a low-income student a voucher that would permit them to choose a public or private school for their education?

And yet, opposition to school choice is vehement and comes from many education bureaucrats and teachers' unions. Note the comments of Walter Hinojosa, legislative director of the Texas Federation of Teachers. "We're ignoring the real problem of not putting enough money into public schools to bring them up to the level of private schools." He suggests that rather than launching a voucher system, lawmakers in Austin should "file an income-tax bill so we could fund education at the proper level."

That should give you a feel for the mindset of many in the public education bureaucracy in our state capitol. Not only are many of the bureaucrats and unions operating on the assumption that more money will solve the problems, but they ignore the fact that most private schools are able to educate children less expensively than public schools can.

In preparation for starting the Austin Children's Educational Opportunity Foundation (CEO) program, the organizers did a survey of twenty private schools and found that the average annual tuition was $2,300. That is exactly one-half the $4,600 it costs on average for public-school students. Why the great difference?

> **Not only are many of the bureaucrats and unions operating on the assumption that more money will solve the problems, but they ignore the fact that most private schools are able to educate children less expensively than public schools can.**

Opponents of school choice argue that private schools attract brighter students who are easier and cheaper to educate. And yet, how does one explain the success of the Messmer High School in Milwaukee? Clearly, there are problem children who require special programs or assistance to move forward, but they certainly are not responsible for that large a difference in cost.

The real problem is the huge bureaucracy that has grown up around public education, not only in Texas, but throughout the nation. Between 1977 and 1987, administrative staffs grew nationally at a rate two and a half times faster than instructional staff. And in Texas, the state auditor noted in a recent report that "the current system of public education in Texas is inefficient. By 1997, the state could save more than $640 million annually by revising funding policies, changing the structure of districts in Texas, and improving management operations."

Instead of many teachers or school employees being dismissed, retiring, or moving on to another career, they become "administrators." The Houston Independent School District (HISD), the state's largest, employs more than twenty-six thousand full- or part-time workers serving two hundred thousand students. It is one of the city's biggest businesses and the city's biggest bureaucracies.

The assortment of administrators includes one superintendent, three associate superintendents, five deputy superintendents, and thirty assistant superintendents. That does not include the twenty-six executive directors, 175 directors, sixty-one supervisors, thirty-one coordinators, and twenty-one managers. Salaries for administrators range from $31,416 to $84,252, while teacher's salaries range from $24,000 to just more than $42,000.

Not only do many administrators lack managerial experience, but some have no one under them to administer. Giving someone a new title has become a substitute for replacing them. If real progress is to be made in establishing site-based management of schools, then much of the administrative bureaucracy of school districts should be eliminated. What is left should be privatized.

> **A**s part of the process of increasing competition and improving efficiency, we should separate non-instructional from instructional services.

As part of the process of increasing competition and improving efficiency, we should separate noninstructional from instructional services. Noninstructional services would include transportation, safety and security, food services, custodial care, physical plant maintenance, health services, and many extracurricular activities.

Most of these noninstructional services are provided currently by schools on a district-by-district basis. They could be provided cheaper and more efficiently on an area-wide basis by using more competitive bidding. If an individual school could provide the same service cheaper than the area-wide contractor or vendor, then they should have that option. In addition to providing those services more cost-effectively, it would also allow superintendents, principals, and teachers to focus on their primary mission—educating Texas schoolchildren.

## Preparing Our Work Force

Nothing is more important to the economic growth and vitality of our state than the quality of the work force filling the jobs of the future. If that work force is unprepared because it lacks adequate education, training, or motivation, then employers will go elsewhere. We simply cannot let that happen.

The current system of public education in Texas is not delivering value for the dollar invested. Rather than continuing to pour more money into a system that is broken, it's time to fix it. I have proposed a four-point program that includes

1. performance-based funding
2. true site-based management of schools
3. creating competition among schools through choice
4. cutting administrative costs and control by privatizing noninstructional services

If we start rewarding success instead of failure, create real competition among schools, and drive decision making back to the parents, teachers, and principals closest to the problems, we can have a system of public education in Texas that is truly first-rate. Why should we accept less?

# 5

# Making Criminals Pay
# Instead of Paying for Crime

f there is one area in which Texans would just as soon not lead the nation, it is in the area of crime. In the last decade, the crime rate in Texas has risen at a much faster clip than the rest of the country, and the gap is getting wider. In fact, the number of crimes committed per one hundred thousand people in Texas increased by 30 percent from 1981 to 1990, compared to less than 1 percent for the nation as a whole.

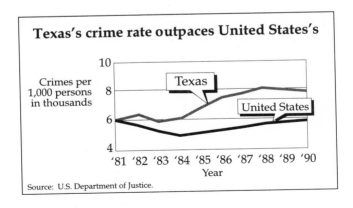

**Texas's crime rate outpaces United States's**

Crimes per 1,000 persons in thousands

Texas

United States

'81 '82 '83 '84 '85 '86 '87 '88 '89 '90
Year

Source: U.S. Department of Justice.

The statistics are even worse if you are talking about violent crimes. The violent crime rate in Texas rose by a whopping 46 percent in the same time period. In 1990, more Texans died of gunshot wounds than from motor-vehicle accidents. Only Texas can claim that distinction. Perhaps the most disturbing aspect of all this is the number of murders and other acts of violence committed by juveniles.

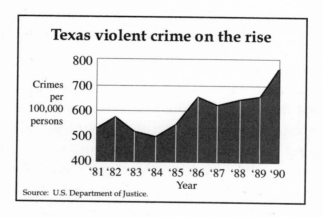

**Texas violent crime on the rise**

Source: U.S. Department of Justice.

As I said earlier, the state's response can best be described as "too little, too late." Officials were slow to respond to the rising demand for prison space, which resulted in cramming more inmates into existing cells. That gave rise to a series of lawsuits, the most notable of which was filed by David Ruiz. The stage was then set for an activist federal judge, William Wayne Justice, to rule that the state prison sys-

**In 1990, more Texans died of gunshot wounds than from motor-vehicle accidents. Only Texas can claim that distinction.**

tem was in violation of the U.S. Constitution.

His court orders made matters much worse by requiring the state to reduce the population of inmates in prison at the very time that criminal activity was escalating. As a consequence, the state has been engaged in a game of "catch-up," feverishly building new prison cells while at the same time releasing convicts who have served only a tiny fraction of their time.

> **I**s it any wonder that criminals consider the slogan "Don't Mess With Texas" a joke? They figure that they can commit crimes in this state with impunity and seldom, if ever, pay the price.

Policies such as parole and "good time," which were once used as rewards for inmates who behaved themselves in prison, now are used primarily as a means of pushing prisoners out the back door. They figure that they can commit crimes in this state with impunity and seldom, if ever, pay the price.

The abuse of the parole system is a case in point. Parole was originally intended as an incentive for convicts who were model prisoners and showed signs of rehabilitation. Most state convicts are eligible for parole after serving only one-third of their maximum sentences. But in the past few years, parole has become the principal means of population control available to state prison officials and has resulted in thousands of dangerous convicts being released early.

The policy of "good time credit" has also been abused. Under the present good-time system, a prisoner earns thirty days off his or her sentence for every thirty days of good behavior. Once again, this good-time credit was created to encourage good behavior from inmates while in prison. If they violate a prison rule or commit a new crime, they are supposed to lose their good time credit. But that is not how it has been working.

Take the case of Raul Meza. In 1982, Meza pleaded guilty to the rape and murder of an eight-year-old Austin girl and was sentenced to thirty years in prison. He collected more that twenty years of good time while in prison and became eligible for parole. However, he was caught with a makeshift knife and violated other rules prompting prison officials to take his good time credits away.

On June 21, 1993, Meza's good-time credits were restored and he was released on parole after serving only eleven years. Not only was his early release a miscarriage of justice, but restoring good time credit to a prisoner who violates prison rules makes a mockery of the entire system. Meza's case was better publicized than most, but it is not that unusual.

In the 1993 regular session of the Legislature, additional prison cells were authorized for construction bringing the total to 107,000 by 1995. Moreover, a new penal code was enacted establishing clearer priorities on eligibility for parole. Violent offenders must serve at least half their sentence or thirty years, whichever is less, and criminals convicted of capital offenses must serve a minimum of forty years.

Those are steps in the right direction, but they will not significantly increase public safety for three reasons.

- First, as explained previously, the prison population is predicted to grow much faster than the availability of new cells.

- Second, we cannot afford to build and operate the number of prison cells it would take to completely end the early release of prisoners. The Texas Criminal Justice Policy Council estimates that it would require *an additional 184,000 cells* at a cost of $5.5 billion in construction and $3.3 billion in annual operating costs.

- Third, juveniles who are the primary driving force in the growth of crime, are largely unaffected by the legislature's actions. Therefore, an effective attack on crime requires a combination of making the current criminal population pay dearly for their deeds, and slowing the growth of that population before the costs overwhelm us.

## Cracking Down on Criminals

L et's start with making criminals pay dearly. Eliminating parole for violent offenders until they have served at least half their sentence is good, but it doesn't go far enough. Most jurors are shocked and horrified to learn that only a small part of the sentences they gave criminals will actually be served. While telling jurors how much of a sentence a convict is likely to serve would be enlightening, it could prompt many juries to double or triple the sentence so that the convict would spend sufficient time in prison. A better approach is for the jury to make the criminal serve the correct sentence and for the state to carry it out. That is what we must work toward.

> **M**ost jurors are shocked and horrified to learn that only a small part of the sentences they gave criminals will actually be served. . . . A better approach is for the jury to make the criminal serve the correct sentence. . .

Given the limited availability of prison space, it is absolutely essential that violent criminals—be they adults or juveniles—do meaningful time. No violent act for which a suspect is convicted should go unpunished, or lightly punished. If imprisonment is to be a true deterrent, violent criminals must know they will be put away for years to come.

A second step that should be taken is to shorten the period of time between when the death penalty is given and when it is carried out. Mistakes may occasionally be made in convicting innocent people, and prosecutors must redouble their efforts to eliminate those mistakes.

However, that does not justify endless appeals and inordinate delays in carrying out a sentence. The state and federal governments should require that all death penalties be carried out within a year of exhausting all avenues of appeals.

Congress should also slash funding for the Texas Resource Center (TRC). The TRC is one of twenty outfits nationwide that receive federal funds to see that death-row inmates are guaranteed adequate representation. This is not *before* their conviction, but rather afterward.

The TRC alone receives more than $3 million and spends much of it attempting to undo what a jury of the defendant's peers did. It is an employment agency for death-penalty opponents. If death-penalty opponents want to change the law of the land, they should focus on the legislature or Congress, not the courts. What was once intended as a means of assuring that the judicial process was fair has now become mostly a method for slowing down the process.

> **The state and federal governments should require that all death penalties be carried out within a year of exhausting appeals.**

Nonviolent offenders must be handled differently. They commit mostly property crimes and outnumber the violent criminals by four to one. While they, too, should serve adequate time in prison, they should not replace violent offenders, if space is limited. Moreover, they should be required to learn something other than better ways to commit crimes before they're released.

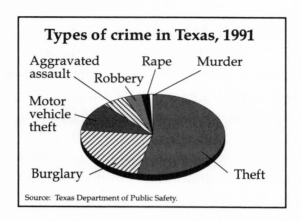

**Types of crime in Texas, 1991**

Aggravated assault — Rape — Murder — Robbery — Motor vehicle theft — Burglary — Theft

Source: Texas Department of Public Safety.

For instance, the average state prison inmate dropped out of school early and reads at about a fourth-grade level. Even if they have the skills necessary to get a job, they know so little about managing their life and communicating with employers, that their chances of getting a meaningful job are minimal. That inmate should not be eligible for release or parole unless his or her reading, communication, and life skills are adequate to apply for, and hold, a full-time job. Indeed, they should be required to earn a certificate to that effect.

That might sound like a tall order, particularly in light of the minimal education and training given inmates in Texas prisons today. And yet, it must be done. How?

108

## Making Criminals Pay Instead of Paying for Crime

Companies all over Texas regularly replace old computers with newer ones. My company certainly has. Instead of mothballing those machines, we should give them to the state to be used in prisons.Instead of mothballing those machines, we should give them to the state to be used in prisons. If that is not feasible, then partnerships should be established with Texas-based computer and electronics companies such as Compaq, Dell, Texas Instruments, and Tandy Corporation. One way or the other, we can outfit our prisons with enough computer equipment, albeit not top-of-the-line.

Companies all over Texas regularly replace old computers with newer ones. My company certainly has. Instead of mothballing those machines, we should give them to the state to be used in prisons.

There are extremely simple and effective computer-based literacy programs that can teach people to read in a fraction of the time required in a classroom. Moreover, the student interacts directly with a machine rather than exposing ignorance to peers in a group. In addition to learning to read, prisoners can also learn job and life skills essential to landing a job once they are released.

I cannot guarantee you that requiring convicts to learn to read will eliminate the likelihood of their committing another property crime. After all, property offenders have one of the highest recidivism rates of any class of criminals. However, I can assure you that the odds of their committing another property crime will be reduced if they have other options available for making money.  It is all part of slowing the growth of the criminal population.

For property offenders who commit their crimes to support drug habits, learning to read must follow breaking their addiction. I am not talking about full-time drug pushers. They fall into the category of violent offenders and should be dealt with harshly. Rather, I am referring to the thief or burglar who is stealing cars or breaking into homes in order to buy drugs.

Texas is in the process of bringing twelve thousand drug rehabilitation beds on-line for convicts who are addicted. That is not nearly enough. More than half of the convicts in state prisons claimed they were under the influence of drugs when they perpetrated their crime. Even though cost is a major impediment to providing more drug-rehab beds for addicted criminals, we must make some tough choices if we are going to reduce the rate of crime in our state.

Earlier, I mentioned that the Texas Department of Mental Health and Mental Retardation (TDMHMR) operated thirteen state schools for the mentally retarded. Due to a federal court order issued in 1983, TDMHMR has been forced to move as many clients as possible out into less restrictive community care  facilities, and to increase the staff-to-client ratio for those who remain. As a result of the increased staff and decreased occupancy of each school, costs have soared. It now costs at least 50 percent more for the highest level of care in a state school as it does to care for the very same client at a private sector facility.

Does the state actually need thirteen schools, particularly if the conditions under which they are currently operating are grossly inefficient economically? No, which is why one is scheduled to close in 1995 and another in 1999. More than two could be closed, but politics and jobs stand in the way.

The parents whose kids are in these schools understandably object to moving their children to a facility that may be hours, rather than minutes, away from home. And the communities in which the schools are located count on the jobs provided as an integral part of their economy. Again, some tough choices must be made.

At least six should be converted from state schools for the mentally retarded to drug rehabilitation facilities for criminals who are addicted. This could add up to forty-five hundred more beds for drug treatment and begin to make a real dent in the state's war on drug addiction and resulting criminal activity. While there is no way to consolidate state schools without upsetting parents, turning the schools into drug-treatment centers would save some jobs, and create many others in the communities affected. Once again, the focus is on slowing the growth of the criminal population by changing the current trends.

The trend which is clearly the most dangerous and disturbing is the growth in juvenile crime, and particularly violent crimes. Gangs and gang-related violence dominate the headlines in most major city newspapers. Three recent incidents in a single month in Houston illustrate the point.

In a suburban park, a bunch of teenagers went on a shooting spree, wounding one seventeen-year-old eight times and injuring six others. A thirteen-year-old boy accidentally shot and killed his girlfriend with whom he was plotting to kill her parents. And six teenage gang members were charged with the vicious strangulation and rape of two young girls who had taken a shortcut home and had happened upon the gang initiating two new members.

One of the gang members, seventeen-year-old Raul Omar Villareal, was heard to proclaim to another, after learning they probably would be charged with murder, "Hey great! We've hit the big time." That kid is a hopeless cause and will be tried for murder as an adult. But there are thousands of others who are too young to be tried as adults and who have totally overwhelmed the juvenile justice system in Texas.

A Houston homicide detective described the problem this way: "We're dealing with a juvenile justice system that still thinks they are handling Dennis the Menace for uprooting Mr. Wilson's flower garden." Indeed, a system that was once intended to deal with nonviolent offenders who commit minor property

112

crimes has instead been flooded with violent offenders.

Once again, the state's response has been "too little, too late." As proof of the slowness with which state authorities have responded consider this: Law-enforcement authorities are not permitted in Texas to take fingerprints and photographs of juvenile suspects, even of felony suspects. A bill to authorize fingerprinting and photographing of juveniles accused of felonies was considered in the 1993 regular session of the legislature, but failed.

Not only are fingerprint and photographic files on juvenile felons nonexistent, but there is no uniform statewide database that allows the exchange among counties of arrest records and other pertinent information. As a consequence, any juvenile offender can run up an arrest record a mile long in one county, then go to another county and start all over again.

We are no longer dealing with a situation in which society attempts to prevent a kid from getting a damaging criminal record for minor acts of vandalism or theft. Rather, we are talking about protecting society from murderers, rapists, and drug-pushers who happen to be fourteen years old.

> A Houston homicide detective described the problem this way: "We're dealing with a juvenile justice system that still thinks they are handling Dennis the Menace for uprooting Mr. Wilson's flower garden."

# Deep in the Heart

In light of these facts, the legislature authorized the collection and exchange of some criminal information among counties regarding juveniles, but you have to wonder why it took so long. The common response for years has been to turn the juvenile offender back over to a parent or parents and let them handle it. But at a time when the family unit has broken down in this country like never before, simply returning a child to the parent or parents is not the answer. That usually is a large part of the problem.

> **The common response for years has been to turn the juvenile offender back over to a parent or parents and let them handle it.**

Experts differ over exactly what causes teen violence, but there are certain risk factors on which most agree. Kids who are raised in a family in which there is child abuse, spouse abuse, or any regular evidence of violent behavior by parents become accustomed to showing their anger or frustration by physical acts.

If a parent has a limited education, no meaningful job, and has kids as a teenager, the chances of those kids growing up to be juvenile delinquents are high. By the same token, the likelihood that those children will learn and accept traditional values is slim. The external pressures and temptations are simply too great.

Pervasive sex and violence on television and in the movies coupled with what they see among their peers encourages kids to engage in both types of behavior without really having any understanding of the consequences of their actions. Parents teaching forbearance, or at least safe sex, must compete with a culture that often portrays virtue and morality as nineteenth-century relics.

Boys who have no father at home, or who have a violent or abusive father, live by the jungle rules of the streets and accept violence as a way of getting what they want. With both guns and drugs, the supply to kids is plentiful and the result is often deadly.

We must come to grips with these facts, not only for our own protection and safety, but also to avoid losing an entire generation of inner-city children to lives of violence, destruction, and hopelessness. We must acknowledge that many of the teenagers who have already committed repeated acts of violence against other people are beyond reasonable hope.

National experts claim that about 10 percent of juvenile delinquents commit 50 percent of all violent crimes. When those kids are arrested, certified to be tried as adults, and convicted, they should be taken out of circulation for as long as a jury thinks appropriate. If that means they are sentenced to spend the rest of their lives in prison, so be it.

The real challenge and hope lies with the nonviolent juvenile delinquent. Today, that kid is largely ignored because whatever state or local resources exist for dealing with juvenile problems are consumed by the violent, repeat offenders. And yet, unless we develop a strategy for handling those kids, they will become the violent offenders of tomorrow.

## Service without the Smile

While various cities and counties have programs aimed at teenagers who may have had a brush with the law, I am convinced that we need a statewide program that offers school and law enforcement authorities a viable alternative for the treatment of these kids. Therefore, I propose the creation of a Texas Service Corps (TSC).

This Texas Service Corps would be created on certain military facilities and bases in the process of being closed or scheduled for closure. It would be operated in cooperation with the United States Armed Forces and the Texas National Guard.

> **This Texas Service Corps would be created on certain military facilities and bases in the process of being closed or scheduled for closure.**

The purpose, very simply, would be to instill values and discipline, build character, and teach the skills necessary to obtain meaningful employment. It would provide physical elements that are challenging without being abusive, difficult without being degrading. Athletic competition among units would be encouraged to build morale. Along with an emphasis on physical conditioning, computers could be used to raise reading and comprehension skills to appropriate levels. All cadets should work toward obtaining a GED as part of graduating from the TSC.

After physical and educational "basic training" would come a focus on appropriate work habits and finally job skills. Early discipline and work habits could be learned through supervised on-the-job training in the construction and repair of roads, bridges, and other infrastructures. Others might concentrate on health care, transportation, and a host of other service-industry jobs.

> **E**arly discipline and work habits could be learned through supervised on-the-job training in the construction and repair of roads, bridges, and other infrastructures.

The goal is to build confidence and self-esteem in these kids through a combination of physical and mental challenges, and to provide them with the skills necessary to lead productive lives. For those who choose to go on to college and could pass the appropriate tests, that would also be an option.

Who would be able to join? The TSC would be targeted to at-risk and low-income males and females ages twelve to eighteen. There would be two levels of entry. The first would be for those who were, in effect, drafted. The second would be for those who enlisted.

"Draftees" would consist of referrals to the program by state or local authorities. The majority would come from juvenile and law enforcement authorities following sufficient evidence of delinquent behavior or trouble in school.

"Enlistees" would include those who voluntarily joined as an alternative to conventional education or who had some history of juvenile delinquency but were not referred to the program by a state or local authority. Rank and privileges in the TSC would be established by performance and behavior.

TSC cadets who complete physical and educational basic training, followed by adequate job skills work, would be eligible to graduate. The idea is to create a sense of personal accountability while building a feeling of belonging—a substitute of sorts for the family structure and discipline so lacking in many families.

Who would operate the program? The army is undergoing a force and end-strength reduction that will result in the elimination of six combat divisions. It is from these units that a very high level of quality leadership and training expertise could be gleaned.

Those who choose to participate in the Texas Service Corps, or any other comparable program in another state, might be placed in a new personnel category with the army reserve. With federal approval, they could earn credit towards twenty years of service, which entitles military personnel to retirement benefits. This would provide a powerful incentive for military personnel to help run the TSC, and it would also help offset the loss of military payrolls in areas where bases are being closed.

Why the military? There is no other institution in America which has the track record of building character and teaching technical skills to men and women of varied backgrounds like the United States Armed Forces.

Military facilities and bases scheduled for closure or conversion, coupled with National Guard and Reserve unit facilities, should provide the appropriate physical space for establishing several different TSC units.

How would such a program be funded in these tough economic times? It would require a commitment of federal, state, and local money from *existing* sources, as well as a new source of funds soon to be available.

As part of the national demobilization of the military, and conversion of some defense contractors to civilian purposes, a transition program aimed at softening the economic impact of these changes has been enacted in Washington. Funds for this will be carved out of the defense budget, and Texas, with its abundance of military facilities and defense contractors, should be eligible for its fair share.

In terms of existing funds, there are several sources. At the federal level, in addition to the defense-conversion funds, the National Guard is encouraged to participate and invest in local programs, the U.S. Department of Justice has funds for innovative law-enforcement efforts, and the U.S. Department of Labor administers a variety of job training programs. Indeed, under the Job Training Partnership Act (JTPA), Texas will receive more than $230 million in 1993. While most of that is already committed to ongoing activities, some could be earmarked for the TSC.

At the state level, the Texas Youth Commission (TYC) has primary responsibility for offenders who are too young for the adult criminal justice system. They operate several detention facilities and counseling programs with a biennial budget of $82 million. In 1992, there were 2,131 youths committed to TYC facilities. A little more than one-third of those kids were committed for violent crimes, and the TYC will spend upwards of $30,000 on counseling and rehabilitating some juveniles.

Like most state programs, funding is based on numbers rather than results and accountability is nonexistent. The Texas Service Corps would represent an attractive alternative for many of the TYC's nonviolent clients.

For those kids who entered the program with drug or alcohol problems, funds should be made available from the Texas Commission on Alcohol and Drug Abuse. According to the TYC, almost half of the kids in their facilities are drug or alcohol dependent, which is one of the most compelling reasons to get them off the streets. Were it not for the need to support a drug or alcohol habit, and the resulting diminished judgment, many of these kids would not be the fearless criminals they seem to be.

# Making Criminals Pay Instead of Paying for Crime

In terms of local funds, every major county in the state expends enormous law enforcement and judicial resources catching teenage offenders, and then turning them over to juvenile authorities or turning them loose. An investment by these counties in taking these trouble-makers off the streets and placing them in the Texas Service Corps would be well worth it. Counties should have the right to contract with the TSC to take custody of certain juvenile offenders for fixed periods of time. Those counties would not be required to pay the full cost of a particular juvenile's involvement, but rather a portion of that cost.

That is by no means a complete list of possible funding sources, but it should give you an idea of the options currently available. Finding the right mix of federal, state, and local funds will be a challenge, but it is a manageable one. The key is to structure a program that ties funding to results, allows the private sector (both for-profit and nonprofit) to participate fully, and keeps decision making in the hands of field officers rather than government bureaucrats. In short, there must be accountability built in at every step of the way.

What we are doing is creating an alternative life path for thousands of delinquent youths. It is too early to tell how many will actually be helped by this program. However, one thing is clear: the price of doing nothing is unacceptable. The Texas Service Corps represents a bold attempt to do things differently and alter the lives of both law-breaking as well as law-abiding citizens in our state.

## Adult Accountability

I constantly cite the lack of accountability in state government programs, and the failure to base funding on results or performance rather than political needs or numerical inputs. The adult criminal-justice system in Texas not only lacks accountability, it has no central focus of responsibility for waging an effective war on crime.

The state shares that responsibility with more county and local authorities than you can shake a stick at. Indeed, developing a coordinated statewide strategy among so many different players and interests would rival getting all the relevant parties in the Bosnia-Herzogovina conflict to agree to a peace plan. Nevertheless, we must press ahead.

Here are the givens:

- **POINT:** Local authorities will continue to control the arrest, trial, and sentencing of criminals in Texas.

- **COUNTERPOINT:** State authorities will control the imprisonment, length of time served, and conditions for release.

- **POINT:** Local authorities will blame the state for the overcrowding of county jails and the early release of state inmates.

- **COUNTERPOINT:** State authorities will blame counties for sending too many offenders to the penitentiary instead of alternative sentences.

All this bickering will do absolutely nothing to enhance public safety and is likely to get worse in 1995.

You will recall that in the absence of adequate state prison space, county jails have been warehousing state convicts until there is an opening at the state level. The counties now receive $20 or $30 a day for each prisoner and they can use the money for anything. Beginning in September 1995, the state will have a legal duty to accept these inmates within forty-five days of completing paperwork. Failure to do so will result in another lawsuit prompting the state to pay even more to county jails.

In effect, the legislature has created another entitlement program with increased costs bearing no relation to the quality of the job anyone is doing. In this case, counties stand to make money by forcing more state prisoners into the pipeline than the state can accommodate. That is why formulating a statewide strategic criminal justice plan is so essential.

All relevant parties must be at the table and the eventual solution must be ratified by the legislature and the governor. For the plan to be implemented successfully, and for a clear determination of success or failure to be possible, performance goals and objectives must be developed. The legislature could tie sufficient funding to those goals to reward success, or penalize failure.

Typically, what gets measured gets done, and what is not measured is often ignored. By focusing all parties on common goals and performance targets, much of the existing friction in the system can be eliminated.

> **In effect, the legislature has created another entitlement program with increased costs bearing no relation to the quality of the job anyone is doing.**

Two other pieces to the criminal justice puzzle require further discussion: schools and parents. The cheapest way to fight crime is to prevent it. Most schools already teach the dangers of drugs and alcohol, but more must be done. For instance, in the Los Angeles public schools, they teach peaceful ways of resolving conflicts starting in the third grade. Much more of that must be done across the country, and particularly in Texas.

Other cities consider the shock approach. Either show children a film which graphically depicts the consequences of crime, or take them to a state prison and let them see it first hand. Of course, in Texas, depending upon the time of day, the kids are just as likely to see prisoners watching television as working. In any event, the best time for intervention, according to national experts, is between elementary school and junior high.

# The Mentor Approach

An approach which we know works, and can be targeted at kids who are thought to be high-probability juvenile delinquents, is mentoring. Boy Scouts, Boy's Clubs, and Big Brothers all seek to provide mentoring and positive role models to boys and young men. Their female counterpart organizations do likewise. However, far too many kids are falling between the cracks. Each school needs a set of volunteer mentors who are willing to take on children headed for trouble. Often a single adult who truly cares about a child will do more to keep that kid on the straight and narrow than any other approach.

Where schools make a tragic mistake is in their handling of certain students who are troublemakers. Although these troublemakers should not be allowed to disrupt the education of other students, expelling them from school often seals their fates as juvenile delinquents. A better approach is to get them out of the classroom and into a program with other disruptive and dysfunctional kids. There, a higher premium would be placed on discipline and order. With the benefit of a little more one-on-one help, many of these kids can regain some of the ground lost and will no longer feel the inadequacy that often prompts disruptive behavior.

## Extending the School Year

For the past several years, many educators and public officials have recommended that the school year be extended. The argument is that there is insufficient time to cover all the material adequately in a nine-month year and that students lose learning momentum over the summer.

While I have always been intrigued with the idea, I have never understood how we could afford a longer school year when we can barely afford the one we have. Nevertheless, there is an additional reason to revisit this issue. When you ask law-enforcement leaders what could be done to deal more effectively with the juvenile problem, many will suggest two things:

- First, keep the schools open from 8:00 A.M. to 5:00 P.M. for the full calendar year. It keeps kids off the streets and out of trouble.

- Second, enlist older people in teaching values and helping build character. It's hard to imagine how foreign these concepts are to some of these children, and, unless they develop some moral compass to guide them through life, they will be lost. The traditional family unit can no longer be expected to impart these values, and churches, which were once the anchor of every community, are struggling to reach these kids.

Many advocates of prevention claim that you have to start even earlier than elementary school. They contend that if a child fits a certain profile at birth, you can predict pretty accurately whether he or she will lead a productive or unproductive life. I think there is a great deal to be said for that and will examine it more carefully in the context of reforming welfare.

I started this section by suggesting that we make criminals pay, rather than taxpayers continuing to pay the bill for crime. In order to achieve that goal, we must put teeth back into punishment, particularly for violent offenses, and slow the growth of the criminal population.

> **Despite our best efforts to improve government's response to these problems, we must also redouble our commitment to strengthening the family.**

My plan would build on the progress made by the legislature in both the construction of new cells and the reform of the penal code. It would further separate violent from nonviolent offenders and see to it that violent offenders served meaningful time.

With respect to nonviolent offenders, it would require them to learn to read as a condition of release and it would increase the number of beds committed to drug and alcohol rehabilitation. Finally, for juvenile delinquents, I have proposed taking the violent repeat offenders off the streets for years to come, and focusing our efforts on nonviolent juveniles who would benefit from doing a hitch in the Texas Service Corps.

Despite our best efforts to improve government's response to these problems, we must also redouble our commitment to strengthening the family. As a father of three children, I know firsthand that there is simply no substitute for a strong marriage when it comes to raising children. I know, as well, that not all marriages work and that we must do more to support single-parent households.

Government cannot legislate good, strong marriages or stable, intact families, but it can adopt policies that encourage both. In the next section on welfare, I will make some specific proposals to do just that.

# 6

# "Ending Welfare As We Know It"

President Clinton likes to say he's going to "end welfare as we know it." I hope he is serious, because so much of the welfare machine is controlled by Washington that we will need its help fixing it.

When I think about my four years on the board of the Texas Department of Human Services, two of them as chairman, I remember certain successes and certain disappointments. The successes included innovative programs to help more welfare recipients find jobs and to prompt coordination among agencies with overlapping responsibilities.

The disappointments came mostly from the lack of progress in shaking up the state welfare bureaucracy and the failure to have sufficient impact on the growth of the welfare population in Texas. It was not for lack of trying.

I was responsible for the first outside-management audit of that huge bureaucracy in more than twelve years, and a waiver from the federal government that allowed Texas to start a year early on moving more welfare recipients into jobs. But implementing the management changes recommended in the audit was fought tooth and nail by bureaucrats who are more intent on protecting their turf than improving services to the clients and saving taxpayers' money.

As a consequence, I have concluded that more dramatic changes are necessary in both the welfare bureaucracy and the rules of the game. If we are going to change the current patterns of behavior, Band-Aids and baling wire will no longer suffice. We need radical surgery. Here are the five elements of my plan to revolutionize human services in Texas:

- Make welfare a short-lived experience by placing two-year limit on benefits.
- Stem the tide of out-of-wedlock births among present or future welfare mothers.
- Establish greater responsibility among men for children they father and families they abandon.
- Refocus resources on strengthening the health, nutrition, and development of preschool kids.
- Shake up the welfare bureaucracy by privatizing functions.

Although the overwhelming majority of people on welfare are children, eligibility is based upon the financial condition of a head of household. In Texas, more than 97 percent of those heads of households are women. About 30 percent of those women are on the welfare rolls for one year or less. They are generally the more motivated, educated, and employable individuals. They are not the problem. Welfare, for them, is what it should be—a safety net to be used temporarily until they can get back on their feet.

Another 18 percent are on welfare for thirteen to twenty-four months, giving us a total of about 48 percent who are on welfare for less than two years. Any limit of two years on eligibility would not hurt those folks. However, there is another 52 percent who have been on welfare for more than two years and almost half of them have been on the rolls for *six years or longer.*

Few, if any, long-term welfare recipients can read at better than a fourth-grade level, nor do they have any skills that would make them employable, except in the most menial job. Indeed, most are so unacquainted with the work world that they lack the experience and confidence to even answer a want ad or fill out a job application. Before going to work, they must learn basic life-survival skills, like how to use public transportation, how to open a bank account, and how to groom and dress properly.

Given the time, expense, and effort it would take to assist these folks, there is a tendency to target the limited education and job-training resources on people who are easier to help. But that just perpetuates dependence on welfare. If we are going to change the pattern, we must force initiative on the part of long-term recipients.

The best way to do that is for the state, over a twelve-month period, to remove every welfare recipient who has been on the rolls for two years or more. The only way to get an extension is to attend any one of a number of programs that will eventually lead to a job. Although education and job training opportunities may be limited, parenting classes and survival skills courses should not be.

It would be phased in over an appropriate period of time to ease the transition. The alternative is to continue to tolerate the long-term dependence that has created a permanent under-class of citizens in this country. That is a great disservice to the recipient, their children, and the taxpayers of this state.

Another aspect of welfare which must be confronted head-on is the ominous growth of out-of-wedlock births. In 1950, according to the Census Bureau, only 3 percent of the births in this country were illegitimate. In 1960, that figure was 4 percent. By 1992, the number had increased to a stunning *24.2 percent*. The figure is highest among African Americans at 67 percent, followed by Hispanics at 27 percent and Anglos at 17 percent. This explosive growth in out-of-wedlock births has helped drive the number of welfare recipients up sharply in the last ten years. Not only do more single mothers become eligible for welfare, but also the size of the monthly benefit increases for every additional child in a family.

In some states, that increased payment might be considered an incentive for having more children, but not in Texas. Anyone who moved to Texas thinking they were going to "make out like a bandit" on welfare was badly misinformed. In our state, the maximum monthly cash benefit for a family of three is $184. Therefore, adding a new child to the family would only increase the benefit by about $61 a month.

No, money is not the primary motivation for Texas welfare mothers to have more babies. Rather, it is an extraordinarily tragic cultural trend that has developed. It is a cultural trend that has taken hold among some affluent, professional women, as well as poor, unemployed women. However, when illegitimacy is coupled with the deep-seated poverty that exists in most inner-city neighborhoods, kids born into those families have a great deal to overcome.

The problem has become such a dominant national concern, that *The Atlantic* magazine reported the following in its April 1993 issue:

> After decades of dispute about so-called family
> diversity, the evidence from social-science

This explosive growth in out-of-wedlock births has helped drive the number of welfare recipients up sharply in the last ten years. Not only does it make more single mothers eligible for welfare, but it helps increase the size of the monthly benefit for every additional child in a family.

research is coming in: The dissolution of two-parent families, though it may benefit the adults involved, is harmful to many children, and dramatically undermines society.

Although government cannot prevent illegitimate births, it can adopt policies that discourage or penalize such behavior. Today, government policies are, at best, neutral, and some would claim, supportive. That must end. What we need is a policy that penalizes the mother, but not her child. We must also find a way to give that mother more hope.

The state should notify all welfare mothers that if they have another child out-of-wedlock, their monthly cash benefit will be reduced by 30 percent and the difference will be made up through in-kind support for the new child only. In other words, the mother would have her cash benefits cut, but would receive coupons that could only be used for infant formula, baby food, bottles, diapers, etc. The child would also be eligible for Medicaid from the first day. Both placing a two-year limit on eligibility and penalizing more out-of-wedlock births would require permission, or a waiver from the federal government. That is where President Clinton's commitment to end welfare as we know it will be tested. At the same time that we're discouraging out-of-wedlock births, we must also find ways of rewarding mothers who do not add to their family. One way is to give them priority access to education and training programs that will lead to a job.

## Find the Fathers

Having dealt with the mother who adds another child while on welfare, we must simultaneously pursue the fathers of those children. The Texas Attorney General's office is responsible for enforcing the child-support statutes in this state. That office has recently announced a program to identify the fathers of illegitimate children while the mother is in the hospital.

A confidential process should be set up to establish paternity. Once that is established, a mandatory contractual arrangement should be made with the man to pay child support. Failure to do so should result in suspension of any license granted by the state, including temporary loss of a driver's license. It is absolutely essential that the fathers of illegitimate children begin to understand that there are serious consequences for their actions.

The fourth component of my proposal to reshape human services in Texas deals not with limitations, penalties, or sanctions, but with saving the children. They are the innocent victims of parental neglect and cultural decadence. At a minimum, we must see to it that they have the nutrition and health care needed to develop a good, sound body. The mind is another matter.

The type of developmental experiences a young child has depends to a great extent on choices made by the parent or parents. For instance, if the mother of a

135

child was born into a family in which drugs or alcohol were prevalent, there is a good chance that pattern will be repeated. And if child care for the mother was haphazard or nonexistent, that could also be repeated.

For most young couples, regardless of education and income, classes in parenting can be extremely helpful, but this is particularly true of young welfare mothers. As a condition of eligibility, I would require that all welfare mothers complete a parenting course within the first month of the birth of their child, if not before. Such a course would provide important information on a variety of topics including proper nutrition, health care, child care, and early educational development.

> $\mathbf{T}$he type of developmental experiences a young child has depends to a great extent on choices made by the parent or parents.

One of the chronic problems facing social service agencies is the lack of coordination among the different providers. Often a mother who is eligible for assistance will not receive it because of the difficulty in getting into the program. In Houston, a working group of public and private sector representatives who have a stake in child care and education is developing a project to better coordinate these services. We want to improve both the quality of the services available and their accessibility.

I serve as co-chairman of a volunteer committee that is spearheading this project. One option they are considering is to analyze the risks confronting a newborn child based upon the education, income, and experience of the welfare mother. If that child is considered to be at high risk in terms of receiving adequate nutrition, health, and developmental care, then a volunteer would be assigned to the mother. That volunteer would serve as a mentor or counselor for the mother, to see that the child got proper care. Such a mentor could be instrumental in helping the mother be a good parent, complete her education, and get a job.

We must find more creative ways to help preschool children so that by the time they enter school at age six, they are not struggling to overcome so many disadvantages. Whether you talk to educators, social workers, or law enforcement personnel, they all agree on the importance of starting to help low-income children early.

The fifth and final element of my plan to revamp human services in Texas involves the bureaucracy. As I mentioned earlier, my efforts at the Texas Department of Human Services to reorganize its bloated headquarters staff were resisted from the first day by those more interested in protecting their turf than improving efficiency. Because most bureaucrats know that volunteer board members serve limited terms,

> **B**ecause most bureaucrats know that volunteer board members serve limited terms, they often engage you in a war of attrition in which they "wait you out" until your term is up.

they often engage you in a war of attrition in which they "wait you out" until your term is up.

Given the entrenched nature of these bureaucrats and the difficulty in firing people under the state-employee rules, it is no wonder that many lose sight of whom they work for and whom they are supposed to serve. Once again, what we need is accountability, and the best way to get it is by paying for performance and creating competition.

If the state were to start privatizing or contracting out certain functions previously performed by bureaucrats, and the contracting party were to perform those functions at a much lower cost and with greater efficiency, it would have a dramatic effect. It could lead to further privatization, and the potential loss of a job by bureaucrats unable to compete. Those are the kinds of programs needed to get their attention.

For that reason, I would recommend contracting out a major staff function of the state welfare agency, specifically, the determination of eligibility of welfare recipients. Social workers should focus more on developing plans to help clients escape welfare than filling out reams of paper to verify their eligibility and access.

Through competitive bidding, private-sector contractors can be given incentive bonuses for low-error rates and for improved automation of the process. A similar arrangement already exists with respect to the administration of Medicaid in Texas. That contract is held by Ross Perot's former company, EDS.

## "Ending Welfare As We Know It"

One of the nation's most extensive experiments in competition between the public and private sectors took place in Phoenix, Arizona. Facing a serious tax revolt, the city contracted out garbage collection to the private sector. The city's Public Works Department was also given a chance to bid. The city auditor carefully examined each bid. Three times the Public Works Department bid, and three times it lost to private contractors. The losses were humiliating and forced the Public Works Department to rethink the way they did business.

They put their heads together and finally came up with some innovations. A new program was implemented giving the employees 10 percent of the savings generated by their suggestions for improvement, up to $2,000. The department's costs came down, and when the next big contract came up for bid, the public employees won. Morale soared because they had proven themselves. The private companies quickly adopted some of the public employee cost-saving ideas and the competition continued to find more innovative ways of bringing costs down.

The City of Phoenix then tried to create competition in other governmental services. The important distinction is not public versus private, it is monopoly versus competition. City Auditor Jim Flanagan summed it up best when he said, "Where there is competition, you get better results, more cost-consciousness, and superior service delivery."

That is precisely what we need throughout state government starting at the Texas Department of Human Services. Paying for performance, creating competition, and moving decision making closer to the customers or taxpayers are all essential elements of establishing greater accountability in government.

> **The important distinction is not public versus private, it is monopoly versus competition.**

Placing a two-year limit on welfare eligibility, imposing penalties on welfare mothers who have more children out of wedlock, and making fathers of these children pay child support are all part of establishing more *personal* accountability or responsibility. It is strong medicine, but necessary if we are going to turn welfare on its ear and start doing things differently in Texas.

## Summary

I have proposed a series of far-reaching changes in public education, criminal justice, and human services. If they are to be implemented, the legislature must break the chains that currently bind this state and limit our thinking. You will recall that 84 percent of the state budget is driven by entitlement programs, dedicated funds, and court orders.

## "Ending Welfare As We Know It"

Although many of the proposals I have laid out can be passed by simple statute, others will require tackling statutory or constitutional entitlement programs and dedicated funds. Make no mistake, it can be done. What we need is leadership with the courage and determination to make it happen. We do not have that today.

# Part III:

# Reform and Recovery

# 7

# Political and Institutional Reform

I will never forget the day I was campaigning in East Texas and walked up to an old gentleman sitting on a park bench at the town square. I stuck out my hand and said, "I'm Rob Mosbacher and I'd appreciate your vote." He said, "I never vote. It just encourages 'em."

I don't blame him for feeling that way. Anger and frustration with government in Washington and Austin has seldom been stronger, and with good reason. Elective office for most is no longer a public service, it is a lifetime career. Winning reelection has gone from being a major concern to being the dominant, overriding concern of most officeholders.

Once lawmakers decide that they want to keep their jobs at almost any cost, their attitudes change. Instead of focusing on a particular policy goal they might have espoused during their

> **W**inning reelection has gone from being a major concern to being the dominant, overriding concern of most officeholders.

campaign, these officeholders concentrate more on what it takes to get reelected. They attempt to avoid casting tough, controversial votes that might upset some people, and they set about raising campaign war chests to scare off any potential opposition.

Consequently, there is no incentive for politicians in Austin to rock the boat and upset the entrenched special interests, much less the constituents back home. They figure if they keep their heads down and avoid controversy, they will get reelected. That is why you see so few "statesmen" today in Washington or Austin.

The type of reform that this state needs, and that I have recommended, definitely falls into the category of "rocking the boat." For instance, improving the quality of public education by creating competition and implementing school choice will likely send most of the teachers' unions through the roof. Permitting parents and students to select their schools means that principals and teachers will be held more accountable for their work. Schools with good teachers will be rewarded with students and money. Schools with poor teachers will be penalized, or perhaps closed.

Any politician voting to provide school choice might well find the leadership of the local teachers' union out campaigning against him come election time. The same would be true of the special-interest groups surrounding the criminal justice system, the welfare system, and others.

If, as a politician, your overriding interest is to keep your job, then the tendency will be to try to please everybody and avoid creating controversy. On the other hand, if your time in office is limited and you cannot continue to seek reelection to that office, then your attitude will be different. You are more likely to focus on making your mark while you are there, on getting something accomplished. That is why term limitations are so essential to improving the quality of government in Texas and the nation.

# Term Limitations

When I was running for lieutenant governor in 1990, I promised that if elected, I would serve only two terms. As things turned out, I didn't serve any. But that was not an idle threat. I stated that, win or lose, I would continue the fight for this fundamental reform. So, in 1991, I founded Texans for Term Limitations, a bipartisan, statewide organization.

More than a quarter-of-a-million Texas voters, fed up with a bankrupt political process, have since joined the group. We advocate limiting statewide elected officials and members of the Texas Legislature to eight years in office. We also support a six-year limit for members of the U.S. House of Representatives and twelve years for members of the U.S. Senate. Under current law, no politician's term in Austin or Washington is limited, with one exception—the president of the United States.

Public-opinion polls show that more than 75 percent of Texans want term limitations. I think most see it as the first and best step toward retaking control of government. While some contend that this is a latter-day conspiracy on the part of Republicans to move Democrat leaders out of office in Washington and Austin, nothing could be further from the truth. Polls indicate that support for term limits is strong among rank-and-file Republicans, Democrats, and Independents. Also, term limits is not a new concept. It dates back to the earliest days of this nation.

The concept of term limits was part of the Articles of Confederation and was included in half a dozen early state constitutions. Thomas Jefferson, in a letter to James Madison, said he was reluctant to sign the new Constitution because it did not call for "rotation in office"—term limits.

> **P**olls indicate that support for term limits is strong among rank-and-file Republicans, Democrats, and Independents. Also, term limits is not a new concept. It dates back to the earliest days of this nation.

George Washington left office voluntarily as our first president, hoping to establish a tradition of two-term limits for all those who would follow. That tradition was kept until Franklin Roosevelt broke it under the unique circumstances of World War II. However, that led to the enactment of the twenty-second amendment to the U.S. Constitution, limiting presidents to two terms.

In more recent times, term limits have surfaced again. In 1992, voters in fourteen states—including California, Florida, and Michigan—passed proposals limiting the terms of their elected officials. Together, the term limit initiatives passed by an average of more than 68 percent across the country.

I support term limits, not as a way to "throw the bums out," but rather as a means of changing the attitude of those elected to office. I also think limits will inspire new people to run for office, bringing new perspectives and new ideas.

Too many good people sit on the sidelines refusing to run for office because they think they will have to spend years and years in the job to gain a senior position with real power. But with term limits, lawmakers move up the ladder of seniority much more quickly and have the opportunity to chair a committee within just a couple of years. In addition, because so many members would have similar seniority, committee chairs would have to be elected.

Given this opportunity to make a difference in a relatively short period of time, I think we would see more business men and women, engineers, artists, house-wives, and others offer themselves for public service. They would be "citizen legislators" who would offer their talents to state government and then return to their communities to live under the laws they had passed.

That is what our founding fathers had in mind when they organized this representative form of democracy. Finally, term limits would address another critical problem facing us today—the loss of public faith and confidence in our political process and its institutions. While politicians have always been a source of humor and ridicule, it has never been as persistent, nor as bitter as it is today. What goes on in Washington is fodder for every late-night comedian, and characterizations of politicians as a lower form of life go unchallenged.

> **T**here is the feeling that good people get elected to office with the best of intentions, but become corrupted by the system and lose touch with the folks they were elected to represent. Term limits is an effort to keep those lawmakers in touch with their roots and improve the quality of representation we get while they are in office.

There is the feeling that good people get elected to office with the best of intentions, but become corrupted by the system and lose touch with the folks they were elected to represent. Term limits is an effort to keep those lawmakers in touch with their roots and improve the quality of representation we get while they are in office.

As popular as term limits are with the voters, it is equally unpopular with elected officials. During the last regular session of the Texas legislature, our group pushed bills to limit terms at both the state and federal levels.

Although ultimately we were defeated by the entrenched politicians, a proposal to limit the terms of state office-holders received seventy-seven votes out of a possible 150 in the House of Representatives. Because we were seeking to amend the Texas state constitution, a two-thirds vote, or one hundred votes, was needed for passage.

Nevertheless, we forced legislators to vote on the record on term limits and they will now have to answer to their constituents as to how they voted and why. Rest assured that those who voted against term limits will have to face this issue in the 1994 campaign.

During the often rancorous debate on the House floor, one irate opponent of term limits rose to ask the sponsor of the bill just what was she trying to fix with term limits. "What is wrong with the present system?" he wondered aloud. Obviously, he is a man out of touch with his constituents.

Over in the Senate, another member who has been in office for more than thirty years called the clients of a lobbyist who was willing to help with term limits and threatened to punish them if the lobbyist continued to aid our effort. The arrogance of power is often incredible.

Term-limit opponents like to argue that this proposal would deny the state and nation experienced, talented public servants. Considering our current state of affairs, you have to wonder just what all that experience and talent has given us. If the present system of lifetime, entrenched politicians in Austin and Washington is so

> **I**f the present system of lifetime, entrenched politicians in Austin and Washington is so good, why are public services so bad?

good, why are public services so bad?

As former Louisiana Governor Buddy Roemer put it in support of term limits, "Government ain't brain surgery." It should not take years of service for politicians to figure out how the process works, and if it is taking that long, they probably had no business being there in the first place.

## Battling Bureaucrats and Lobbyists

**A**nother argument opponents like to use is that term limits will make lobbyists and bureaucrats more powerful. Hogwash. Most lobbyists hate the idea of term limits. In California, they contributed $5 million to the campaign to defeat the term-limit proposition on the ballot in 1990. Why? Because lobbyists make their living and build their influence through friendships with elected officials. If limits are imposed, they will have to constantly cultivate new relationships with an ever-changing group of lawmakers. In the absence of being able to influence lawmakers as a result of long-term personal relationships, they will have no choice but to make their arguments on the merits of the issue.

As for bureaucrats taking over, we might already be too late. The truth is bureaucrats already run state government. I do believe, however, that limits could actually help reduce the influence these state employees currently wield. The most incestuous relationships that now exist in government are those between high-ranking bureaucrats and long-term, powerful lawmakers. Here is what I mean:

The state employees hired to head an agency must go before the House and Senate committees that control their funding every two years and justify their requests for more money. That agency head knows that his best hope of getting what he wants is by developing a personal friendship with that committee chairman. It is human nature. The more familiar the two become, the less likely that chairman is to ask the tough questions and insist on accountability. That is what I mean by incestuous. Term limits will create much higher turnover on committees and among committee chairmen, and will cut down on long-term, incestuous relationships.

**L**obbyists make their living and build their influence through friendships with elected officials. If limits are imposed, they will have to constantly cultivate new relationships with an ever-changing group of lawmakers.

As a last resort, opponents will claim that we don't need term limits because voters can throw a politician out of office on election day. The best way to limit a term is to vote someone out of office. That is the way we were

153

taught in civics class that the system is supposed to work. Unfortunately, in the real world, it doesn't happen that way.

More than 90 percent of the U.S. Congress is re-elected every two years. In the Texas Senate, the reelection rate is more than 85 percent, except when a redistricting lawsuit turns things upside down. And in the Texas House, the reelection rate is 91 percent. There is more turnover in the Texas House than indicated by the reelection rate, but it is more a function of people quitting to go back to their businesses than it is a result of competitive elections.

Why are these reelection rates so high at a time when voters are so dissatisfied? Two reasons:

- First, incumbent office-holders have huge advantages over challengers.
- Second, many voters have no real alternative to their incumbent.

It takes tens of thousands of dollars to unseat an incumbent member of the Texas legislature. Defeating an incumbent member of the U.S. House will cost an average of $1 million. Few challengers can muster the war chests necessary to compete effectively, particularly when incumbents can tap the lobbyists for political action committee contributions.

Even when a voter is willing to turn against the incumbent, the alternative is often so unacceptable that the voter has no choice but to return to the fold. Take, for example, the woman who wrote a letter to the editor of the Houston Post. She claimed she was all prepared to vote against her congressman until she discovered that his opponent was a follower of fringe candidate Lyndon LaRouche.

In 1992, voters sent the largest crop of freshman congressmen and women to Washington in decades. Term-limit opponents proudly contend it proves that term limits are unnecessary. Hardly. Out of 110 new members of the House, only twenty-one won their elections by defeating incumbents. The rest resulted from deaths, resignations, retirements, or redistricting.

Term limits are the single most important step that we could take to restore political accountability and offer voters more competitive elections. However, it is not a panacea. It must be part of a comprehensive set of reforms that includes changes in campaign finance rules and the imposition of a tough, common-sense ethics code for elected officials and for lobbyists.

# Campaign Finance Reform

The way we finance political campaigns in this state borders on being criminal. You would be hard-pressed to devise a system that encourages more abuse by special interests and misuse by large contributors. You see, there are no limits on how much individuals or political action committees (PACS) can give to statewide officials or members of the legislature. Therefore, it is not unusual for a profession like personal-injury trial lawyers to contribute cumulatively more than $500,000 to a candidate for governor or lieutenant governor. Indeed, that is what happened in the 1990 campaigns of Ann Richards and Bob Bullock. Is it any wonder that the personal-injury lawyers in Texas feel protected by the governor and lieutenant governor?

In June 1992, I went before the Platform Committee of the Republican Party of Texas and urged the adoption of a package of campaign finance reforms. It was subsequently adopted, and I believe it should become state law. I recommended limits on individuals and PACS of $5,000 for statewide offices, $2,500 for Senate races, and $1,000 for House races.

> **There are no limits on how much individuals or political action committees (PACS) can give to statewide officials or members of the legislature.**

Most politicians don't want to admit that their major contributors have more influence than the small-dollar donors, but they do. If you don't believe it, just look at the top-level appointments made by our state's governors over the last two decades. By and large, the choice political appointments go to the biggest contributors.

That is not to suggest that all recipients of large contributions are inordinately influenced by big givers.

Indeed, many big contributors ask nothing in return and expect nothing out of the ordinary. However, the temptation is great and the perception of impropriety is very evident. We simply cannot afford the appearance of sleaze and corruption in Texas that comes when a contributor is handing out $10,000 checks on the floor of the Senate. It looks an awful lot like government is for sale to the highest bidder.

One other change that needs to be made involves legislators who leave office either voluntarily, or involuntarily. If they become lobbyists, which unfortunately is all too common, they are currently allowed to use their surplus campaign funds to contribute to or buy access to their former colleagues. That is flat wrong. Any and all surplus campaign funds held by a retiring member of the legislature either should be returned to the contributor or turned over to the Texas Ethics Commission to help defray operating expenses.

We will never be able to eliminate completely the corrupting influence money can and does have on our elected officials and government. But by limiting the size of contributions and controlling the use of surplus campaign funds, we are at least removing two of the primary means of abusing the political system currently in practice in Austin. The last component is ethics reform.

## Ethics Reform

During the 1991 regular session of the legislature, no topic was hotter than reform of the ethics code, or lack thereof, that governs business in the state capital. Governor Richards sent lawmakers a thirteen-point plan that she said was the absolute minimum the legislature should adopt.

By the time legislators were finished watering down the original plan, it had only a few of the thirteen reforms she wanted. By then, her attention had apparently moved on to something else and she let the bill become law. If she were really serious about ethics reform, she would have vetoed the bill and insisted on stronger legislation. Perhaps she was satisfied that that was the best she could do, even with a legislature dominated by her party. *I* know we can do better.

> If she were really serious about ethics reform, she would have vetoed the bill and insisted on stronger legislation.

In the interest of open government and full disclosure, candidates for statewide office and the legislature should be required to release their complete tax returns for the past five years. I did this voluntarily as a candidate for lieutenant governor in 1990 and believe it should be law.

Lawmakers should repeal the "we're different from you" laws, such as the one exempting them from misdemeanor arrests during legislative sessions. Nothing infuriates voters more than legislative bodies passing laws that exempt lawmakers from their applicability and the voters are correct. It smacks more of a monarchy or dictatorship than a democracy.

> **W**ith respect to lobbyists, those who are paid to influence legislation should not be allowed to pay for hunting, fishing, or other recreational trips with legislators.

With respect to lobbyists, those who are paid to influence legislation should not be allowed to pay for hunting, fishing, or other recreational trips with legislators. If lobbyists and legislators want to go hunting or fishing together and pay their own way, it is another matter, but no more lobby-paid trips.

Lobbyists should also be prohibited from giving legislators personal gifts. Why, other than attempting to influence a vote or to thank a lawmaker for his vote, would a lobbyist give someone a gift? It is an ancient ritual that needs to be stopped.

And finally, lobbyists should be limited to $250 per person, per year, in entertaining lawmakers. That will pay for plenty of lunches and dinners and represents a reasonable limit.

Term limitations, campaign finance reform, and tough ethical standards are all essential elements of draining the swamp of sleaze in Austin.

Initiative and referendum (I and R) is another desperately needed reform. I believe people should have the opportunity to directly petition their government. The Austin insiders who so vehemently oppose I and R think it gives voters too much control, too much power. They say lawmakers would be abdicating their responsibility to represent and carry out their constituents' wishes if they approved I and R. And yet, if they were genuinely committed to carrying out the voters' wishes, they would have passed term limits already. If politicians are truly interested in restoring public faith and confidence in our political institutions, they should do the unexpected and clean up their own house. Time is of the essence.

## Bringing Method to the Madness of State Government

Leo "The Lip" Durocher played baseball in the major leagues for seventeen years and managed for twenty-four. In his early years with the Brooklyn Dodgers he played and managed, giving rise to a host of colorful tales. One such tale involved a game in which one outfielder after another made errors on simple pop flys and line drives, raising Durocher's temper to a boiling point.

When yet another error was committed, Durocher benched the player involved and flew out of the dugout proclaiming, "I'll show you guys how to play the outfield!" After Durocher also made an error on the first ball hit his way, he stormed off the field, threw his glove on the bench, and said, "You guys have got the outfield so screwed up, nobody can play it!"

I often wonder if Texas state government is too "screwed up" for anyone to make it work. With more than 220 agencies, boards, and commissions, the organization chart of our state government looks more like the wiring scheme on the space shuttle. You could not design a more convoluted organizational plan if you tried. So it is not surprising that the right hand seldom knows what the left hand is doing, and that accountability is missing.

> **W**ith more than 220 agencies, boards, and commissions, the organization chart of our state government looks more like the wiring scheme on the space shuttle. You could not design a more convoluted organizational plan if you tried.

Taking on that mess in a comprehensive way would require a whole other book. But there are several changes that if implemented would bring a greater sense of coherence and purpose to state government and begin the process of reorganization. Let's start with the governor's office.

The two most important powers of the governor under our state constitution are the power of appointment, and the power to veto legislation. Some of the appointments are to fill unexpired political terms such as on a state court, state elected office, or most recently, to fill temporarily a seat in the United States Senate from Texas. These appointments typically last until the next regular election, or in certain cases, the next special election. Governor Richards's appointment of Mary Scott Nabors to fill the seat of Lena Guerrero on the Railroad Commission is an example of the former. Her appointment of Bob Krueger to replace Senator Lloyd Bentsen is an example of the latter. While those appointments were highly visible, particularly in light of the controversy surrounding Guerrero and Krueger, they are not the most common.

The more common appointments a governor is called upon to make are to executive boards and commissions charged with running virtually every department and agency of state government. All governors want to appoint their people to implement their agenda, assuming they have one. The problem is that the terms for these boards and commissions do not run concurrently with the term of the governor. Therefore, the governor must wait to fill vacancies as they become available on a rotating basis.

For example, I was appointed to the board of the Texas Department of Human Services by Governor Bill Clements in January 1987 to serve a six-year term. I was elected chairman of the board in January 1989 and could have continued to serve as chairman until January 1993. Despite the fact that Richards replaced Clements in 1991, her team would not have control of that board until two full years into her term in office. That doesn't make sense. That's why I stepped down. Now compare that to service in the executive branch in Washington.

Imagine what our federal government would be like if cabinet officials—such as my father, who served as secretary of commerce in the Bush administration—continued serving until two years into the Clinton administration. It would give a whole new meaning to the term gridlock.

Although departments and agencies in Texas were meant originally to have more independence and autonomy than those in Washington, you cannot establish real accountability in state government unless a governor can take control from the first day in office. Therefore, I would recommend we employ a little common sense. Let's make terms of all appointees to major boards and commissions run concurrently with the term of the governor.

> **L**et's make terms of all appointees to major boards and commissions run concurrently with the term of the governor.

There are so many positions to be filled that some will end up spending another six months to a year on their board, but at least the governor should have the option of replacing them from the first day. The next challenge is making the disparate departments and agencies work better together. Today, there are no rewards or incentives for various agencies to coordinate their efforts or cooperate with each other. As a consequence, coordination is rare. Let me offer an example.

Drug and alcohol abuse is a direct cause of a variety of problems facing this state, including the growth of crime, juvenile delinquency, child abuse, welfare dependency, and homelessness. The state agencies that deal with the problem include the Criminal Justice Administration, Department of Human Services, Texas Education Agency, the Health Department, the Texas Youth Commission, the Mental Health and Mental Retardation Department, the Commission on Drug and Alcohol Abuse, and others.

> **O**nce a department or agency gets its funding from the legislature, or from a dedicated fund, its members are off like the Lone Ranger doing their own thing.

During my tenure on the board of the Department of Human Services, there was never a single meeting of the various agency board chairmen and staff heads to discuss a common strategy for fighting drug and alcohol abuse in Texas. There may have been an occasional statewide conference involving all the usual suspects, but there was no ongoing intergovernmental mechanism for addressing this problem. Once a department or agency gets its funding from the legislature, or from a dedicated fund, its members are off like the Lone Ranger doing their own thing. If we are going to bring a sense of coherence and accountability to state government that must change.

The governor should establish a cabinet like structure involving the chairmen and top staff officer of each of the major agencies in the state. The governor should chair it, and the lieutenant governor and speaker of the house should serve as vice chairmen. The purpose of this cabinet committee

> **G**overnor Richards set up an interagency committee at the beginning of her term, but it was only at the staff level and has had little impact on coordination.

would be to meet weekly to identify issues of concern to the state and plot a coherent, coordinated strategy for dealing with them. Such a committee would allow the governor to make assignments, allocate responsibilities, and hold agency leadership accountable for performing.

Governor Richards set up an interagency committee at the beginning of her term, but it was only at the staff level and has had little impact on coordination. I am not proposing that we reconstitute state government into cabinet departments, but rather that the external and internal leadership of the major agencies meet regularly with their counterparts axzznd with the senior elected leadership of the state. Such a process might have everyone singing off the same sheet of music for a change.

# Let's Downsize

The next step that needs to be taken is a major reduction and consolidation of state departments, agencies, and commissions. Texas has at least twice, and some would say five times, as many agencies as it needs, and the bureaucracy continues to grow. Since Ann Richards took office as governor, the state has added an incredible twenty thousand more bureaucrats.

Several years ago, the legislature set up the "Sunset Commission" as a means of periodically requiring each agency to justify its existence. It wasn't long before the lobbyists and constituencies associated with each agency mastered that process and began to dominate it. As a result, after years of sunset review, the impact has been minimal. They did manage to kill the Andrew Jackson Memorial Commission (after it was apparent that it had not met in years) and the Pink Bollweevil Commission. In short, the process has been a bust.

What Texas needs is a commission with the independence and expertise to recommend which agencies should be phased out and which should be continued or consolidated. Such a commission should consist of individuals selected by the governor, lieutenant governor, and speaker of the house, and modeled after the Defense Base Closure and Realignment Commission set up by the Congress.

That commission was structured in such a way as to overcome the natural political resistance to ever closing a military facility in the United States. By conducting an open process in which all interested parties have a full opportunity to be heard, and then making recommendations that are very difficult to overturn, the commission is succeeding in accomplishing what many considered politically impossible. A similar process could be applied in Texas.

I would recommend that a commission be appointed for the purpose of reviewing approximately one-third of the state government departments, agencies, boards, and commissions per biennium. In other words, given the enormity of the task, it should be broken into thirds based upon function. Recommendations would be made on that third of state government to the legislature at the beginning of the next three regular sessions. For instance, all health and human service entities might be considered in the first phase, education and training entities next. All dedicated funds associated with a particular agency or function should be considered at the same time.

Following the example set by the Defense Base Closure and Realignment Commission, extensive public hearings should be held to give all interested parties a chance to testify. Once conclusions have been reached, they should be submitted in a single package to the legislature. Recommendations to phase out or consolidate an entity could only be overturned by a two-thirds vote of the legislature. Such a super-majority would place an appropriate burden of proof on the supporters of that agency. Today, that burden is on those who want to kill an agency, and they are seldom as well organized or financed as the supporters of that entity.

> **What clearly does not work is breaking big bureaucracies into smaller pieces without establishing new measures of performance and accountability.**

The goal of the process is to improve efficiency, eliminate needless bureaucracy, consolidate functions into fewer agencies, encourage greater coordination of services, and last, but not least, save the taxpayers money. It is a tall order, but a manageable one if the commission is constituted properly and takes on state government one piece at a time. Once again, leadership at the top is essential to making this happen.

What clearly does not work is breaking big bureaucracies into smaller pieces without establishing new measures of performance and accountability. A case in point is the agency with which I was associated, the Texas Department of Human Services. While there are an abundance of changes that should be made to that huge agency, many of which were identified in the management audit that I prompted, Governor Richards's approach is different.

With her support, various Department of Human Service programs will be moved to a new Department of Public Health, and others will go to the new Department of Protective and Regulatory Services. The former De-partment of Health will disappear, and its programs will be absorbed by the other three agencies. Although each agency will have its own Board, all three agencies will be governed by a new Health and Human Services Commission that will also have its own commissioner. Sound complicated? Here is the bottom line: Since these functions were reshuffled and the departments reorganized, the number of bureaucrats working on these programs have risen from 23,065 to 27,543, an increase of 4,478 since 1991. We need to take a different approach.

# 8

# Building a Business
# Climate Second-to-None

As we approach the twenty-first century, there is no state in the union better positioned to prosper than Texas. As a result of the 1980s economic downturn, the Texas economy is more diversified and more competitive than ever. Sitting on the border with Mexico affords us the opportunity to serve as the gateway to expanded trade, not only with our neighbor immediately to the south, but with all of Latin America. International trade is where the future potential growth is for Texas.

According to the U.S. Department of Commerce, Texas leads the nation with $18.8 billion in exports to Mexico, and it will keep growing, particularly with approval of the North American Free Trade Agreement (NAFTA). Indeed, Texas will gain more from that agreement than any other state in the country. One study estimated that more than one hundred thousand net new jobs would be

> **International trade is where the future potential growth is for Texas.**

created in Texas before the end of this decade, so long as trade barriers continue to come down.

Although some low-skill, low-wage jobs will move south of the border with the free-trade agreement, it should be pointed out that those jobs have been leaving the United States for many years for Korea, Taiwan, and other Pacific Rim nations. Why not encourage their movement to Mexico where they not only provide badly needed employment for Mexican workers, but also reduce the incentive for illegal immigration?

Mexico will be infinitely better able to tackle its own labor and environmental problems if its economy is expanding and creating jobs. In short, the problems that some Americans like to decry in Mexico would only persist, or get worse without NAFTA. With NAFTA, Mexico can deal with its own problems more effectively. In the meantime, Mexico is buying *70 percent* of all its imports from the United States and the challenge for Texas is how to make the most of that trade.

So far I have spent the better part of this book detailing the case for dramatic change in state government. If we hope to maximize our economic potential, we must get control of state spending and establish accountability for tax dollars invested. As I have mentioned repeatedly, we need a work force that is well-educated, well-trained, and highly motivated—but that is not all.

There are two other major areas that require our attention if we hope to realize our full potential:

- The first involves increasing the availability of capital for small- and medium-sized businesses.
- The second entails reducing the number of needless, abusive lawsuits.

More than eight out of every ten net new jobs created in Texas for the foreseeable future will be created by small- and medium-sized businesses. A Fortune 500 corporation that moves its headquarters to Texas will generate more publicity, but the real engine of economic growth is supplied by small businesses, many of which employ ten people or fewer.

> **T**ight credit, ever-expanding legal liability, and unaffordable health insurance are all felt more acutely by small business than large.

For too long, our state and federal governments have paid only lip service to small business. After all, small businesses cannot afford their own office or individual lobbyists in Austin or Washington, so they are reduced to working through trade associations. And although such organizations do their best, they end up spending most of their resources on preventing bad things from happening rather than successfully promoting positive measures.

The problems facing small business are similar to the problems facing all business, except more so. Tight credit, ever-expanding legal liability, and unaffordable health insurance are all felt more acutely by small business than large. Although both state and federal government can impact these problems, the one area in which the federal government is likely to have the greatest impact in the short term is health care.

Depending upon how that debate unfolds, a national program to expand access to health care can either be a blessing for small business or a curse. If the final package approved by the Congress imposes new, costly mandates on all businesses, it could be fatal for many small businesses. Only time will tell.

The two problem areas where state government can be more helpful are the availability of capital and the abuse of our legal system.

## Increasing Capital Availability

Despite some of the lowest interest rates in recent memory, borrowing money to start a small business is difficult, if not impossible. Borrowing money to *expand* a small business is only slightly easier.

The Small Business Administration (SBA) attempts to help, but it often runs out of money before the fiscal year is half over. Moreover, many businesses will never seek SBA loans because of the stigma attached and perceived red tape.

What Texas needs is its own initiative to encourage conventional banks to do more small-business lending. A number of states have such programs, but none is better than the one in Michigan. The Michigan Capital Access Program was enacted in the mid-1980s as part of an ambitious economic development effort.

The program represents a business-government partnership in which private financial institutions are encouraged to make loans that just fall short of being "bankable" under conventional criteria. Such loans might be assigned to this program, requiring the borrower, the lender, and the state all to contribute something to a special loan-loss reserve fund set up at the participating bank.

> **W**hat Texas needs is its own initiative to encourage conventional banks to do more small-business lending.

Here is how it works:

If I wanted to borrow $100,000 for my business and a participating bank concluded that I had insufficient collateral for the loan, the bank could refer my loan application to the Capital Access Program. In so doing, they would assess me a fee of between 1.5 and 3 percent for originating the loan. The bank would then match that fee and the state of Michigan would match the contribution of the borrower and lender combined. In other words, if I were charged a 2-percent fee, the bank would add 2 percent and the State of Michigan would put in 4 percent, for a total of 8 percent.

The loan-loss reserve fund would be used to cover any potential losses to the bank if the loan were to go bad. Unlike some loan programs in which government bureaucrats are making business decisions about who can borrow money, this program leaves all basic lending decisions to banking professionals. In fact, all the bank must do in order to secure the state's approval, and contribution to the loan-loss reserve, is submit a one-page form showing the size, terms, and nature of the loan. So long as the loan is not made for a prohibited activity, such as purchasing real estate, the state's approval comes within ten days. If borrowers believe they can obtain less-expensive financing elsewhere, they are free to shop around.

Since the inception of the loan-loss reserve fund in 1986, more than twenty-three hundred loans have been made to businesses of various sizes. The default rate is under 6 percent. For every dollar the state of Michigan has invested in the program, it has created at least $20 of private sector credit. Although there is no limit on the size of loans made under the program, there are practical limits dictated by the risk the bank is willing to take and the size of their loan-loss reserve fund. The average size of loans made over the last few years is around $50,000. Consequently, an investment of $6 million from the state of Michigan has created $120 million in bank credit and permitted hundreds of small business loans.

I have spoken at length with Michigan officials responsible for the program, as well as bankers who are familiar with it. The response is favorable. Bankers like it because it is easy to administer, and the state likes it because it provides superb leveraging of limited funds.

Based on that response, I worked closely with former Texas State Representative Barry Connelly to introduce a similar measure in the state House in 1989. With only minor modifications, a bill entitled the Texas Business Enhancement Fund passed both the House and Senate that year. However, like so many programs passed by the legislature, it has never been funded. Although that generally saves the state money, in this case it has cost many small businesses an opportunity to get started or to grow. The time has come to crank it up.

A second area of particular need for increased capital availability relates to trade. In order to take full advantage of the export opportunities in Mexico and beyond, this state must help small- and medium-sized businesses have access to those markets.

The U.S. Department of Commerce has helped develop the National Trade Data Bank which lists thousands of trade opportunities available to American businesses around the world.

The state of Texas also has access to that information. The problem is not so much finding export opportunities once you enter the system, but financing them.

Once again, Texas can take a page from the playbook of another state. In this case, California. Back in 1985, California launched its World Trade Commission's Export Finance Office (CEFO). The CEFO provides working capital loan guarantees to financial institutions for small- and medium-sized businesses involved in export activities. These guarantees cover 85 percent of an export loan up to $500,000.

The key to California's program is that it provides a guarantee to finance the purchase of an export order. In other words, if a company has a firm export order, the California program will help finance the purchase of materials, labor, and services required to do the deal.

The CEFO program guarantees can also be used to extend payment terms to export buyers of California goods and services. The California Assembly appropriated $5 million to secure the loan guarantees, but they seldom use it. In fact, the default rate is less than 1 percent.

> **Why doesn't Texas have a program like that? It does. In fact, it is modeled after the California program. But in classic Texas style, our program is the proverbial "all hat and no cattle."**

Through a combination of interest earned on the funds in the program and fees paid by participants, that $5 million has increased to $7 million. Since 1985, CEFO guarantees have backed up more than $800 million in export sales. It is now responsible for about $100 million a year in exports, and it should increase to $200 million in the near future.

Why doesn't Texas have a program like that? It does. In fact, it is modeled after the California program. But in classic Texas style, our program is the proverbial "all hat and no cattle." The Texas Export Finance Program was enacted as part of the Texas Department of Commerce back in 1989. It suffers from two serious problems:

- First, the Texas program is invisible. They have no money for marketing and consequently are not on the radar screen for most exporters looking for help.

- Second, the Texas program is underfunded. It has only $2 million and most of that is used in transactional financing for a relatively few deals. Although that $2 million can be leveraged into some $16 million in economic activity, that is in a state that does $50 *billion* in export business.

If we are truly committed to helping small- and medium-sized businesses in Texas participate fully in the expansion of trade with Mexico and elsewhere, we must staff and finance the Texas Export Finance Program adequately. Also, we must aggressively market the program so that more small exporters can take advantage of it.

The Texas Business Enhancement Fund and the Texas Export Finance Program share much in common. They both are modeled after successful programs in other states, and they both leverage a very modest investment of state resources into a much more significant sum of economic activity. And yet in Texas, neither program has received the support necessary to make it a viable option for most businesses. It is high time these programs are funded adequately before more opportunities to create export-related jobs are lost.

## Reforming the Legal System

I seldom mention this, but in the interest of full disclosure, I must admit I was educated to be a lawyer. Although I passed the Texas bar exam, I have not practiced law a day in my life. I simply felt the education was important.

In the last ten years, having a law degree has been an invaluable asset in the business world. Barely a day goes by in our business that we are not required to carefully consider some complex legal issue. Sadly, questions of legal liability and exposure heavily influence where we do business and what kinds of business we are willing to do. It is not a matter of doing something intentionally wrong because we are proud of our reputation as honest, straight-shooting members of the oil patch. Rather, it is a question of what kind of risk is there for some enterprising lawyer to use as the basis for filing a frivolous or harassing lawsuit.

I was at a meeting of oil-industry leaders in which the pros and cons of international exploration and production were under discussion. Since so much of the continental United States has already been explored, many in our industry have begun to drill more wells in other parts of the world. One industry executive was asked which of the many foreign countries where they were operating did they consider the political risk the greatest. Without hesitating, he answered, "California!" Given some of the huge jury awards made in this state, he could have said Texas.

**Texas is considered one of the most litigious states in the country. Six of the ten highest-paid trial lawyers in the United States practice in Texas and in 1991, three of the ten largest judgments in the nation were won in Texas.**

Texas is considered one of the most litigious states in the country. Six of the ten highest-paid trial lawyers in the United States practice in Texas and in 1991, three of the ten largest judgments in the nation were won in Texas.

A legal system which is supposed to dispense justice often looks more like the "Wheel of Fortune." Just look at the size of some of the prizes: A Dallas jury awarded $120 million to a former executive of a company for his claim of wrongful termination. A Galveston jury awarded the former bondholders of a disbanded company $550 million because they had allegedly been misled by the company's auditors and investment bankers.

The Texas House Business and Commerce Committee concluded in an October 1992 report on excessive jury awards, that "Texas is widely recognized in the business world as a plaintiff's forum and one which should be avoided at all costs."

How did Texas develop this reputation and what has been the economic impact? Dr. Bernard L. Weinstein of the University of North Texas did an excellent study for the Texas Public Policy Foundation and the Center for Lawsuit Reform. In it, he laid out several reasons for the image of Texas as a plaintiff's forum.

First, the nation has become increasingly litigious. With the expansion of the tort system, lawsuits are no longer viewed as a last resort. The rising number of practicing lawyers, coupled with the removal of restrictions on lawyer advertising have both contributed to the growth in litigation.

In Texas, the ranks of lawyers have increased 57 percent since 1980 compared to a 22-percent growth rate for the state's population. This apparent "glut" of attorneys has spawned fierce competition for business and the use of media advertising to find clients. In 1992, Texas lawyers spent $88 million on various forms of print and electronic media advertising. Personal injury lawyers accounted for 85 percent of that total.

The tendency of many plaintiffs' trial lawyers to accept cases on a contingency fee basis and to seek astronomical punitive-damage awards, enhances the inevitability of litigation. Moreover, juries seem willing to use the judicial process to redistribute income from seemingly wealthy individuals or businesses to supposedly injured parties. The cost of their "generosity" is quite high.

Dr. Weinstein estimates that the direct cost of the "tort tax" in Texas is about $12 billion each year. When you add to that the indirect costs associated with concerns about litigation, it probably exceeds $25 billion a year. Such indirect costs include both lost business opportunities and sharply higher insurance premiums.

The business area most directly affected is manufacturing. It is estimated that some 110,000 industrial jobs have been lost in Texas in the last decade. This is for a variety of reasons, including concerns over product liability, the cost of workers' compensation, or the unwillingness to build something innovative and different that might give rise to a slew of lawsuits. Some businesses shut down, while others simply moved out of state.

For instance, Lennox International, a manufacturer of air conditioners that moved its corporate headquarters to Texas ten years ago, closed a huge production facility in Fort Worth and moved the six hundred jobs to other states. There is no telling how many other businesses abandoned plans to move to Texas or to expand a plant here.

Not only has the litigation explosion hurt manufacturing, it has also driven up the cost of health care in Texas. Doctors, nurses, and health-care facilities, hoping to avoid malpractice lawsuits, resort to defensive medicine as a means of protecting themselves. Weinstein estimates that cost at around $702 million per year.

**There is no telling how many other businesses abandoned plans to move to Texas or to expand a plant here.**

Although it should come as no surprise, tort claims cost this country about $185 billion a year. When you wonder what some of the competitive differences are between the United States and Japan, look at what American businesses spend on limiting their liability compared to the Japanese. And when comparing the costs of health care in the United States to other industrialized countries, ask what their doctors spend on malpractice insurance. Simply put, this country in general, and this state in particular, must come to grips with this legal crisis.

In 1987, the Texas legislature enacted some modest tort reforms, but they did not go nearly far enough. In the 1993 regular session of the legislature, further progress was made on one issue—product liability. Senate Bill 4 passed, containing a provision protecting innocent retailers, wholesalers, and other distributors from product-liability lawsuits if they played no role in the design or manufacture of the product in question. Once again, it was a step in the right direction, but much remains to be done.

The reforms recommended by Weinstein and the Texas Public Policy Foundation fall into four categories: enact more tort reform, improve the handling of civil procedures, alter the rules on lawyer advertising, and change the way we choose judges. I concur in all their recommendations. Let's start with tort reform.

## Deep-Pocket Defenders

The reason most lawyers sue a long list of defendants in personal-injury cases is because they are hoping to find a "deep pocket" in the bunch. That is legal slang for a defendant with money. If the plaintiff's attorney can establish joint and several liability, then the wealthy defendant could end up being responsible for the entire judgment despite being only partially responsible for the wrong committed. In other words, if the defendant who was primarily responsible is broke—under joint and several liability—all other parties must help pay the judgment. That encourages a broad search for "deep pocket" defendants and dramatically increases the risk to everyone doing business. There are several potential remedies for this apparent injustice:

- Joint and several liability should be abolished, as it has been in several other states, or it should only be allowed to help cover actual economic damages incurred.

- Separate the establishment-of-liability phase of the trial from the consideration of punitive damages. By so doing, the financial condition of the defendant would not be a consideration in any determination of fault.

185

- A third idea that I like is requiring that all punitive damages be paid into the general revenue of the state government, rather than into the pockets of lawyers.

Another top priority, which would fall under the heading of more tort reform, involves the Deceptive Trade Practices Act in Texas. It was passed with the intention of permitting consumers to recover triple damages from sellers who engaged in deceptive trade practices. However, with the general expansion of tort liability, it now allows suits among a variety of professionals for what would ordinarily be described as honest, unintentional mistakes. The statute needs to be clarified and restricted in its focus.

And finally, under the tort-reform umbrella, the legislature must resist any efforts to retreat from the workers' compensation reforms enacted in 1989. Although those reforms have been ruled unconstitutional by a court of appeals in San Antonio, the case is on appeal with the Texas Supreme Court.

## Making Sense of Civil Cases

A second category of reform consists of improving the process by which civil cases are handled. "Time is money" in most businesses, but particularly in the legal profession in which attorneys are paid by the hour. The prospect of a company having to pay lawyers for hundreds of hours of defense work often is more frightening than actually losing the case. Plaintiffs' lawyers understand that concern and use it to their advantage to force settlements, despite the merits of the lawsuit.

In order to reduce the cost of litigation and distribute that burden more equitably, several changes should be made. We should follow the lead of Arizona and enact a statute that streamlines the process and more strongly encourages alternative means for resolving disputes.

The elements of such a statute would include

The prospect of a company having to pay lawyers for hundreds of hours of defense work often is more frightening than actually losing the case. Plaintiffs' lawyers understand that concern and use it to their advantage to force settlements, despite the merits of the lawsuit.

- limits on "discovery," (the process by which evidence is gathered in advance of the trial)

- judicial discretion to penalize lawyers or clients who engage in "unreasonable, groundless, abusive or obstructionist conduct"

- requirements for arbitration in certain smaller cases. In Arizona, if litigants who appeal a decision from arbitration fail to increase the original award by more than 20 percent, they must pay double the legal costs of their opponents.

The results from the Arizona law have been positive. Costs for both sides have fallen by as much as one-third, the number of discovery motions has dropped by 90 percent, and the list of small cases resolved by arbitration has skyrocketed. We need the same statute in our state, not only to reduce the costs of litigation, but also to help "unclog" the courts.

## Questionable Advertising

The third area requiring immediate reform is legal advertising and the solicitation of clients. My secretary was recently involved in an auto accident in which she was rear-ended at a stoplight. Not long after the accident report was filed, she received seven separate letters from lawyers offering to help her. Each letter urged her to "protect her rights" and "get what she is entitled to" under the law. Consultations are free and no fees must be paid unless and until a recovery is made. In other words, they work for contingency fees of up to 33 percent.

As one who attended law school in the 1970s and has been an inactive member of the Texas bar for more than fifteen years, I think this advertising is a disgrace. I realize that with a surplus of lawyers, many must compete for business to make a living, but there must be a better way than preying on the innocent victims of auto accidents, or folks who lived near toxic-waste site, or people who live under high-voltage power lines, and the list goes on.

Solicitation of clients is against the law, although the line has grown fuzzy. Some lawyers disregard it altogether. The following is a true story that occurred in Texas recently. As Sergeant Joe Friday on "Dragnet" used to say, "The names have been changed to protect the innocent."

Case in point: A worker claimed he slipped on the deck of a vessel in Corpus Christi Harbor. He filed suit against the owner and operator of the vessel and

> **I realize that with a surplus of lawyers, many must compete for business to make a living, but there must be a better way than preying on the innocent victims of auto accidents.**

sought damages. After a year in which very little progress was made, an alleged witness of the incident went to the operator. He said the victim had offered him a percentage of the money won in court if the witness would testify that oil on the vessel had caused the accident.

But the witness now wanted to cut a better deal. "I will be straight about it," he told a company representative. "I want $100,000 in cash, in small bills." For the money, he would recant his eyewitness testimony.

The company went to the police. At a second meeting between the alleged eyewitness and another company employee, a police wiretap captured the extortion plan and the witness's threat to kill the employee and his family if this scheme was reported.

The company suspected, but could not prove, that a lawyer representing the alleged victim was behind the whole thing. In any event, the witness was indicted for two felony offenses—witness tampering and retaliation. He pleaded guilty, and got ten years of probation—a mild slap on the wrist.

That might seem like an extreme example, but it is proof of the sorts of scams and games that are being played to generate work for lawyers and to give them access to outrageous jury awards. Although only a tiny fraction of the practicing lawyers in this state engage in such conduct, the activities of a few damage the reputations of all.

It is incumbent upon the Texas bar to deal aggressively with the loss of public faith in this profession. Outlaw advertising, deal more harshly with solicitation, place much greater emphasis on alternative means of dispute resolution, and recommend that all punitive damages go to the state rather than into the pockets of seemingly greedy lawyers.

The final area of needed legal reform in our state relates to the selection of judges. Texas is one of only nine states that continues to select judges by partisan elections. What makes matters worse is that many judicial campaigns are financed almost entirely by lawyers and there are no limits to the size of campaign contributions.

In 1992, Democratic Supreme Court candidates received 57 percent of their $2.5 million in campaign contributions from trial lawyers. The Republican candidates received less than 1 percent of their $3.4 million from them. In fact, in the highly publicized race between incumbent Oscar Mauzy and challenger Craig Enoch, Mauzy received $878,814 from trial lawyers, compared to only $1,050 for Enoch.

CBS "60 Minutes" reporter Mike Wallace interviewed Mauzy in 1986 and asked, "Is Texas justice for sale?" Mauzy defended the practice of judges accepting large contributions from lawyers practicing in their courts, and he finally paid the price when Enoch defeated him in 1992. In truth, the practice is indefensible. Even if a judge can claim that his or her judgment is unaffected by a siz-

> **E**ven if a judge can claim that his or her judgment is unaffected by a sizable contribution from an attorney practicing in his or her court, the public perception is otherwise. What we are talking about here is public trust.

able contribution from an attorney practicing in his or her court, the public perception is otherwise. What we are talking about here is public trust.

The public wants a judiciary that is qualified, independent, and accountable. There are two ways to provide that. One is to place strict limits on contributions to judicial candidates by lawyers and their firms. The second is to change the way we choose judges.

I would recommend that contributions to appellate judges be limited to $500 per individual and $2,500 per firm. That would cover candidates for the Supreme Court, the Court of Criminal Appeals, and the courts of appeals around the state. Also, I would recommend that contributions to district court judges be limited to $250 per individual and $1,000 per firm. These limits would allow lawyers who know the most about judicial candidates to continue to contribute without having an individual or cumulative impact that is so distorted.

In selecting judges, I generally support the so-called "Texas Plan," which calls for the nonpartisan selection of appellate judges based upon merit. Under this plan, judges would be selected by the governor for a fixed term from a list submitted by a judicial nominating commission. The commission would be bipartisan and include lawyers and non-lawyers.

Once that judge had served his fixed term, he would run in an uncontested confirmation election. I would recommend that he be permitted to serve only one more term. If he received a "no" vote from the public, the vacancy would be filled by the nominating commission.

With respect to district court judges, they should run on nonpartisan ballots. They, too, should have limited terms and be forced to run on their records.

If this state is willing to deal with its legal problems comprehensively rather than in a piecemeal fashion, we can regain the image we once had as a "judicially friendly" state. Otherwise, we will continue to carry this economic burden vis-a-vis other states. Weinstein made the point best when he indicated that in 1981, Texas's manufacturing climate was ranked second in the nation. By 1990, it had fallen to twenty-seventh, due in large part to the growing risk of litigation.

Building a business climate that is truly second-to-none requires that we clean up our judicial act in this state and provide tangible, creative assistance to small- and medium-sized businesses that are starved for capital. It is not enough to simply talk about it in a political campaign. We have to see to it that it gets done.

# 9

# Coming to the End
# of the Road

**W**hen I first began writing this book, I was seriously considering joining the 1994 Texas gubernatorial race. I have since decided against it. Why? One of the reasons is my fervent hope that the arguments I have made in this book will be considered on their merits rather than in the context of a partisan political campaign.

I have sought to describe our problems in plain English and to avoid exaggerating the challenges we face. For the reader who made it from start to finish, it should be abundantly clear that Texas really is at a "fork in the road." We can either continue down the same road traveled for the past fifteen to twenty years and end up deep in some ditch, or we can start to do things differently.

I have laid out a road map for doing things differently, but freely admit that it will take extraordinary leadership and courage. The average Texan is much more preoccupied with the political situation in Washington than with the problems in Austin. That means it could be another three or four years before voters demand the kind of dramatic change in their state government that they are already demanding of their national government. We cannot afford to wait.

There are at least two emotions felt deep in the heart that help define the health and welfare of a society: hope and fear. Today, there is too little hope and too much fear.

Many Texans are without hope of leading productive lives because our educational system is failing them, and our criminal-justice system is intervening too late. The growing cost of this failure already threatens our economic and social well-being. We cannot afford four more years of "Don't Worry, Be Happy" government in Austin.

At the same time, there are many others who are victims of a changing economy and are struggling to start new careers. Will the state be a help or a hindrance in that quest? People need reassurance that the state can help with the transition, or at least not add to their burdens.

The flip side of hope is fear. Today, millions of Texans live in fear for themselves, their families, and their property. Although law-enforcement officials are doing the best they can, violence and bloodshed has become so commonplace that it numbs our senses and prompts us to take matters into our own hands. The debate over carrying handguns is just the latest manifestation of that anxiety.

## Coming to the End of the Road

There is only so much that government can do. Ultimately, individuals and families must take more personal responsibility. However, one thing is clear: We must try to break the cycle of violence early. That is why I recommend concentrating more on preschool children and placing kids headed for trouble in the Texas Service Corps. We simply cannot stand to lose any more control of our streets or neighborhoods.

Also, we cannot continue to tolerate mediocrity or worse in our public-education system. Giving local schools the opportunity to fashion their own education strategy, basing funding on results, creating competition through choice, and privatizing noninstructional services will help educators do a better job. Pursuing the elusive goal of "equity" in funding simply diverts attention from the quality of education available in our schools. We can do better. We just need leaders with the courage and commitment to make changes.

I see no evidence of that courage or commitment among the top elected officials in Austin. The governor spoke proudly of creating a "New Texas" in Austin, but all she has done is appoint different people to oversee the same mess. And although the lieutenant governor receives praise for being one of the few people in state government who can get anything done, he is still trying to figure out how to raise more revenue to pay for the same programs.

The problem in Texas is not lack of money, it is how it is spent. That is the point of this book. Establish accountability, adopt some creative new approaches, and just watch what happens. Texans have always risen to the challenge in the past. I have no doubt that we can do it again.

# Resources

Applebee, Langer and Mullis. *Crossroads in American Education*. Educational Testing Service, Princeton, New Jersey, 1990.

Barthel, Joan "For Children's Sake the Promise of Family Preservation." Philadelphia, Pennsylvania, 1992.

Bingham, Janet. "Charter Schools Blossom, Education to Break out of Old Molds." *Denver Post*, 4 July 1993.

Bouvier, Leon F., and Dudley L. Poston. "Thirty Million Texans?" Center for Immigration Studies, Washington, D.C. 1993.

Broder, David. "Tempting Alternatives, Funding Cutbacks Threaten Nations's Public Schools." *Houston Chronicle*, 10 September 1993.

Chubb, John E. and Terry M. Moe. "Give Choice a Chance in Texas Public Policy Foundation." Texas Lezar, ed., "Making Government Work: A Conservative Agenda for the States." San Antonio, Texas, 1992.

Chubb, John E. and Terry M. Moe. "Politics, Markets and America's Schools." Washington, D.C., The Brookings Institute, 1990.

Copelin, Laylan. "Study: Lobbyists Paid at Least $34.6 million." *Austin American-Statesman*, 30 April 1993, and "Senators Refuse to Restrict Their Law Practices." *Austin American-Statesman*, 29 April 1993.

Craymer, Dale K. "How Texas State Finance Works: Discretionary and Non-Discretionary Funds in the Budget." Presented to the Governor's Revenue Task Force.

Drucker, Peter. *The New Realities*. New York: Harper and Row, 1989.

Fabelo, Tony, Ph.D. Briefing to the Board of Texas Department of Criminal Justice, 18 February 1993.

Honea, Jan. "Validating Self Report Through Technology: Changing Assumptions and Management Implications." *Texas Journal of Corrections*, November-December 1992.

Jackler, Rosaline. "Congress Struggling with Bill to Shorten Death-Row Appeals." *Houston Post*, 24 July 1993.

Kantrowitz, Barbara. "Wild in the Streets." *Newsweek*, New York, 2 August 1993.

Kuhn, Thomas. *The Structure of Scientific Revolutions*. 2d ed. Chicago: University of Chicago Press, 1970.

# Resources

Markley, Melanie. "Parent Power in Schools Grows Awkwardly." *Houston Chronicle*, 4 July 1993.

Murdock, Steve H. and Md Nazrul Hogue. "Demographic and Socioeconomic Change in the Texas Population, 1980 to 1990." Vols I-IV Department of Rural Sociology, Texas Agricultural Experiment Station, The Texas A&M University System in cooperation with The Texas State Data Center, Texas Department of Commerce. (College Station, Texas, November 1992).

Norquist, John O. "A Ticket to Better Schools." *Reader's Digest*, July 1993.

Osborne, David, and Ted Gabler. *Reinventing Government*. Reading, Massachusetts: Addison-Wesley, 1992.

Perelman, Lewis J. "Hyperlearning; Clinton's Greatest Opportunity for Change." Discovery Institute Inquiry, 10 December 1992.

Petersilia, Joan. "Building More Prison Cells Won't Make a Safer Society." *Corrections Today*, December 1992.

Robison, Clay. "Sacred Cow in Texas, Highway Fund Tough to Budget at Budget Time." *Houston Chronicle*, 31 January 1993.

Root, Jay. "Houston Feels Back to the Wall." *Houston Post*, 1 March 1992.

Samuelson, Robert J. "What Limits?" *Newsweek*, New York, 22 March 1993.

Schexnayder, Deanna, and Leslie Lawson. "Texas and U.S. Families, 1990." *Texas Businessweek Review*, Bureau of Business Research, April 1992.

Seib, Gerald F. "Americans Feel Families and Values are Eroding, but They Disagree Over the Causes and Solutions." *The Wall Street Journal*, 11 June 1993.

Shanker, Albert. "Letting Schools Compete." *Northeast-Midwest Economic Review*, 13 November 1989.

Smith, Bob. "Messmer High School: The Road Less Traveled." Milwaukee, Wisconsin, 1992.

Tutt, Bob. "Postwar Legislators Wrestled with School Reform." *Houston Chronicle*, 6 June 1993.

Wahl, Maureen. "First Year Report of the PAVE Partners-Advancing-Values-In-Education Scholarship Program." Milwaukee, Wisconsin, 1993.

Weinstein, Bernard. "The Texas Tort Tax." Texas Public Policy Foundation, San Antonio, Texas, October 1993.

Whitmire, John. "Texas Getting Tougher on Crime, and Smarter About it as Well." *Houston Chronicle*, 20 June 1993.

Whitmire, Richard "Study: U.S. Losing a Generation." *Houston Post*, 22 June 1993.

Will, George F. "Statistics Don't Back Education Lobby." *Houston Chronicle*, 13 September 1993.

# Resources

Wolfgang, M.E., R. Figlio, and P. Sellin, "Delinquency in a Birth Cohort." Chicago, 1972.

Young, Mary Lynn. "Juvenile Justice: An Archaic System?" *Houston Post*, 1 August 1993.

Young, Mary Lynn. "Star-Crossed Paths Reflect Teen Violence." *Houston Post*, 11 July 1993.

Sources for material mentioned in this book also includes various articles, reports and studies published by the E.M. Clark Foundation, *Parade* magazine, Sam Houston State University, San Antonio School Choice Research Project, Texas Research League, Texas Comptroller of Public Accounts, Texas Bond Review Board, Texas Education Agency, Texas Public Policy Foundation, Texas Higher Education Coordinating Board, Texas Department of Human Services, Texas Legislature Budget Board, Texas Criminal Justice Policy Council, Texas Senate Interim Committee on Criminal Justice, Texas Juvenile Probation Commission, Senate Select Committee on the Juvenile Justice System, as well as other various Texas select committees and federal government entities, to include the United States Department of Justice.